Collecting
and
Identifying
Old
Watches

Books by H.G. Harris

Handbook of Watch and Clock Repairs
Advanced Watch and Clock Repair
Collecting and Identifying Old Clocks

COLLECTING
and
IDENTIFYING
OLD
WATCHES

H.G. HARRIS

1978

EMERSON BOOKS, INC.

BUCHANAN, NEW YORK 10511

LIST OF DRAWINGS

LIST OF PLATES

35 Marine chronometer by Brockbanks, London. Circa 1800.

36 Marine chronometer by J.R. Arnold, London. No. 425. Circa 1813.

37 Marine chronometer by Barrauds, London. Circa 1818.

38 Marine chronometer by Breguet Neveu & Cie, Paris.

39 Marine chronometer by Parkinson & Frodsham, London. No. 253.

40 Pocket chronometer Thos. Giffin, London. No. 337.

41 Marine chronometer by Molyneux & Sons, London. No. 1558.

42 Marine chronometer by Winnerl, Paris. No. 441.

43 Marine chronometer by Brockbanks & Atkins, London. No. 1000. 1834.

44 Early 19th century gold cylinder watch by Courvoisier & Cie. No. 5745.

45 Clock-watch movement by Robert Ward, London. Circa 1790.

46 Cylinder escapement watch by Ellicott, London. Circa 1765.

47 Verge escapement watch by Richard Motley, London. Circa 1765.

48 English cylinder escapement movement. Circa 1770.

49 Late 18th century English cylinder escapement movement by John Brockbank, London.

50 Late 18th century English cylinder escapement movement by John Kentish Junior, London. No. 1200.

51 Gold verge watch. Swiss. Circa 1800.

52 Skeleton verge watch. Swiss. Circa 1800.

53 Early 19th century cylinder movement by French, London.

54 Movement of spring detent pocket chronometer by Charles John Cope, London. Circa 1815.

55 English rack lever movement by P. Litherland & Co., Liverpool. Circa 1799.

56 Rack lever movement by Reid, London. No. 6125. Circa 1835.

66 Gold repeater by Moulinie, Bautte et Moynier. Swiss. Circa 1820.

67 Gold tourbillon watch by Jacques Frédéric Houriet, Le Locle. Swiss. Circa 1815.

68 Gold and enamel quarter repeater by Soret & Fils. No. 6601. Circa 1780.

Gold miniature cylinder watch by Prior. Swiss. Circa 1790.

Gold and enamel verge watch by L'Epine à Paris. Circa 1790.

Gold and enamel verge watch by Fres Veigneur à Genève. No. 12804. Circa 1810.

Gold and enamel châtelaine watch by Josiah Emery, London. No. 660. Circa 1775.

Gold and enamel verge watch by Chevalier & Compé. No. 4116. Swiss. Circa 1820.

69 Nine gold and enamel form watches. Swiss and German. Circa 1800-1850.

70 Late 18th century cheap verge watch.

71 Quarter striking verge movement by Daniel de St. Leu, London. Circa 1770.

72 Triple cased verge watch for Turkish market by Isaac Rogers, London. No. 19043. Circa 1792.

73 Triple cased verge watch for Turkish market by Edward Prior, London. Circa 1800.

74 Quarter repeater by Blondeau, Paris. Circa 1835.

75 Equation watch by L'Epine.

76 Gold cylinder watch by Robert Melly et Cie. à Genève. No. 2020. Circa 1820.

78 Gold lever watch by Breguet. No. 4684.

Gold cylinder watch by Le Roy. No. 114. Circa 1820.

Gold cylinder watch by Breguet. No. 4419. Circa 1826.

81 Fake Breguet repeater. Circa 1820.

LIST OF COLOR PLATES

Plate I

Gold and enamel lyre form watch.
Gold and enamel beetle form watch. Circa 1800.
Gold and enamel mandolin form watch. Circa 1800.
Gold and diamond ring watch.
Gold repeater with châtelaine.
Gold and enamel basket form watch. Circa 1800.

Plate II

Gold and enamel automaton repeater. Circa 1830.
Enamelled musical box with watch. Circa 1820.
Gold and enamel watch by Ilbery. No. 6249. Circa 1800.

Plate III

Enamelled striking watch by Pe Dutens. No. 571. Circa 1750.
Gold and enamel watch by Patron. Circa 1770.
Gold and enamel watch by Bovet. Circa 1840.
Gold and enamel watch by Valentin. Circa 1780.
Gold and enamel watch.

Plate IV

Gold and enamel repeater. Circa 1800.

Gold and enamel watch. Circa 1810.

Gold and enamel watch. Circa 1790.

Gold and enamel watch by Barrauds. No. 9673. Circa 1820.

Gold and enamel watch. Circa 1800.

Gold and enamel watch by Veigneur. No. 12084. Circa 1790.

Plate V

Gold and enamel watch by Tompion. Circa 1710.

Gold and enamel astronomical watch by Godon.

Gold montre à tact by Breguet. No. 608. Circa 1800.

Gold and enamel harp form watch. Circa 1810.

Gold and enamel automaton.

Gold and enamel pistol form watch. Circa 1800.

CONTENTS

Preface

THE first mechanical clocks appeared about 1280 but well over two more centuries elapsed before watches were invented. During the last century there has been an active world-wide market dealing in antique clocks, but it is only in relatively recent years that such a widespread interest has been taken in antique watches.

Books have been written on the subject, some of which are now regarded as classics, but many are now unobtainable and, unless one is fortunate enough to find a second-hand copy, one has to rely on their being available in public lending libraries or at the excellent library owned by the National Association of Watch and Clock Collectors.

The aim of this book is to fill a great need by providing a basic knowledge of the development of watches from the time they were first introduced in about 1500 until about 1830 which is the time when mass production methods were introduced, first in Switzerland and then in America. Generally, watches prior to 1830 were individually made.

Among the early settlers in America were watchmakers from Europe. These men found little or no demand for their skills, but in any case it was almost impossible for them to make watches owing to lack of facilities and materials. The majority of existing American watches were made after 1850.

There are four main groups among those actively engaged in antiquarian horology: the private collector, the dealer, the auctioneer and the repairer. For those readers who wish to combine financial gain with the enjoyment of an engaging hobby, then buying and selling is the answer. It means that whenever the opportunity presents itself one should visit second-hand shops, market stalls, junk shops, bazaars, pawn shops, and anyone who might possibly possess old watches. I once visited an old established furniture shop that sold new and second-hand pieces and found that over the years the proprietor had put to one side all the watches he had found in drawers of old furniture that had been purchased for resale. Many of those watches proved to

15

be collectors' pieces.

The value of an old watch will depend on its age, the maker, the type of watch, the extent of its complicated work, and its general condition. Usually, the older it is the greater is its value. If the maker is well known, then that in itself will be of interest to a collector or dealer. A movement fitted with complicated work is almost invariably a better selling proposition than a plain watch, particularly if it is in good working order.

Even so, never reject at first sight any watch merely because it shows signs of damage or being incomplete. A watch in that condition could be of great interest to a collector if, for example, it bore the signature of an eminent maker, or had some singular historic interest.

Having acquired an old watch one should be extremely cautious before handing it to a restorer or repairer. Unless the work can be carried out under proper conditions so that the finished result is as the original would have been, it is better to leave it alone. It is a mistaken belief that a going watch has a greater value than one in need of repair. The real value lies in the originality of the piece and it is usually wiser to leave the watch as it is unless you have access to a workshop where these specialized skills are employed.

Assessing the value of an old watch requires experience. It follows, therefore, that a beginner must seek the advice of someone competent in this field such as an accredited dealer.

I am left now only with the hope that within this book you will find sufficient interest and information to enable you to make a start with what may well develop into an exciting search for collectors' pieces. I wish you every success.

H.G. Harris

CHAPTER 1
The Pioneer Watches
(1500-1600)

THE first watches ever made appeared in Germany between 1500 and 1510 and are believed to have been the work of Peter Henlein, a Nuremburg locksmith (1480-1542).

The only information we have about these watches has been obtained from various documents that were written early in the sixteenth century and are now in the care of museums and private collectors.

At that time mechanical clocks had been in use in Europe and England for more than two hundred years. Made by blacksmiths and erected in abbeys, cathedrals and churches, these large medieval iron turret clocks were driven by large weights hanging from the ends of ropes. Striking was controlled by a locking plate.

This situation continued until the latter part of the fifteenth century at which time there was a demand from wealthy families for small domestic clocks. This demand was met by the manufacture of iron Gothic chamber clocks, mostly made by locksmiths, but again hanging weights were employed as the driving force.

No one knows how and when the coil spring was invented but it is a fact that about 1470 Italy produced the first spring-driven clocks. This invention provided a new form of mechanical energy hitherto unknown, and its application to clocks, as an alternative to hanging weights, resulted in timepieces becoming portable.

The Italian clockmakers appear to have underestimated the importance of their idea because it was left to the clockmakers of Germany to exploit this new source of motive power.

At the beginning of the sixteenth century spring-driven clocks appeared in Nuremberg made in the shape of a drum. They had cylindrical cases and stood flat on a table with the circular dial uppermost. The earliest dated clock of this type known to exist was made in 1525 by Jacob Zech of Prague for Sigismund I, King of Poland. The case is nine and three-quarters inches in diameter. It was a matter only of development before these clocks were made small enough to be worn or otherwise carried on the person.

This transition was in part accomplished by Peter Henlein when he made small round drum-shaped clocks about two and a half inches in diameter. They were too small for use as domestic clocks and too large and heavy to be worn about the neck. Most probably they were intended as travelling clocks to be carried in a bag. This possibility is supported by the absence of pendant rings. Peter Henlein also made spherical-shaped pendant watches to look like musk-balls used for carrying perfume.

Of the few early watches that have survived almost all are German, the majority of which are to be found in museums, and it is for this reason that the sixteenth century can offer a collector little more than a historic background to the beginning of watchmaking. Nevertheless, this knowledge makes a worthwhile contribution in helping to appreciate the subsequent stages in development.

Although Germany was first in the field of watchmaking, France was a very close second. In 1518 Julien Coudray, clockmaker to Louis XII and Francois I, was making watches in the French town of Blois. After him came Jehan du Jardin and Guillaume Coudray, both of whom were clockmakers to the royal court. The industry developed and the town prospered until, by the late sixteenth century, it became the center of the watchmaking industry in France.

In the Louvre, Paris, is a spherical pendant watch. It is the oldest known French watch and was made in 1551 by Jacques de la Garde. There is another similar watch made by him in 1565 that now belongs to the Maritime Museum, Greenwich, London.

During the sixteenth century Germany produced more watches than France but the quality of workmanship was not up to the standard of the French. It was not until about 1590 that France increased its output, and from that time they slowly pulled away from Germany and eventually took the lead about the middle of the seventeenth century.

There is no knowledge of watches being made in England before

1580, and the few that were made at the end of the sixteenth century were copies of German cases with typically French dials and fusee movements.

It is believed that Bartholomew Newsam, one of Queen Elizabeth's clockmakers, made a few watches. A large clock-watch carrying the initials BN in the Metropolitan Museum of Art, New York, is most probably by him.

Movements

The principle of operation of those early European spring-driven clocks and watches is similar to that of the medieval clocks; i.e. a source of energy was used to drive a train of three wheels, one of which turned an hour hand, while a verge escapement governed the rate at which the train was allowed to run. The important difference was the employment of a coiled spring to provide the motive power instead of using a hanging weight.

The verge escapement, Fig. 1, consisted of a crown wheel and a verge. The crown wheel was cylindrical with triangular-shaped teeth cut at one end. The verge was a thin rod with two pallets spaced at a distance equal to the diameter of the crown wheel. The angle formed by the pallets was a little over eighty degrees.

The verge was mounted centrally across the mouth of the crown wheel and secured to one end was a balance. This took the form of a foliot, rather like a dumbbell in appearance, or a wheel, which supplied the mass balance necessary to govern the speed of the escapement. The dumbbell was almost invariably confined to German watches until about 1625, whereas the wheel, which appeared about 1575, was more usually found on French and English watches.

The force of the spring tried to drive the train of wheels but the verge escapement held the train in check. When a crown wheel tooth met a pallet the tooth pushed the pallet forward and clear, and the tooth escaped. At that moment the tooth diametrically opposite encountered the other pallet and the sequence of movement was repeated.

When a pallet was moved by the crown wheel the balance was swung in a semi-rotary direction, and when the other pallet made contact with a tooth the inertia in the balance gave recoil to the crown wheel.

In Fig. 1 (inset) tooth C is pushing against pallet A causing the

19

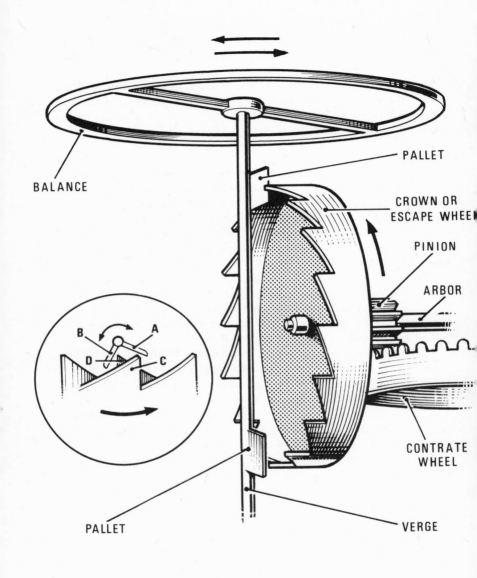

Fig. 1. Verge escapement with wheel-type balance.

20

verge to turn counter clockwise. When tooth C escapes, the crown wheel continues to rotate until tooth D is halted by pallet B, but the verge still retains some of its mass balance impetus and it pushes against tooth D causing the crown wheel to recoil.

The power in the mainspring then takes over and tooth D pushes against pallet B causing the verge to turn in a clockwise direction. When tooth D escapes from pallet B the cycle of movement is repeated, and each time a tooth escapes, the crown wheel turns and then recoils. Meanwhile, the balance continues to swing first in one direction and then in the other.

The makers of the early Italian spring-driven clocks soon found that whereas the mechanical energy stored in a hanging weight remained constant throughout its fall, such was not the case with a coiled spring. When the spring was fully wound it exerted maximum force, but as the spring unwound so the energy contained within it became progressively less causing the movement to slow down and lose time.

The rate of timekeeping of a verge escapement varies considerably with any change in driving force, and even in clocks where the force of a hanging weight was constant, the verge proved to be a notoriously bad timekeeper. The introduction of coiled springs with their inability to provide a constant force made the early watches even less reliable than their predecessors.

Clearly some form of compensation was required and about 1475 the Italian clockmakers introduced a very successful device called the fusee, Fig. 2, probably invented by Leonardo da Vinci. It took the form of a conically shaped pulley, with a continuous spiral groove, that was fixed to an arbor, one end of which was squared for winding and the other end of which was free to rotate in a plate. The fusee was positioned close to a mainspring drum-shaped barrel which was free to rotate about an arbor held stationary by a ratchet wheel and click. The inner end of the coiled mainspring was located on the arbor, and the outer end was hooked to the side of the barrel. Attached to the large diameter at the bottom of the fusee was one end of a length of gut that was wound round the outside of the mainspring barrel.

When the fusee was turned by the winding key the gut was transferred from the barrel to the fusee causing the barrel to rotate. This wound the spring until the stop work arm, mounted on the fusee, arrested further rotation and prevented overwinding.

When winding was complete, the tension in the mainspring caused the barrel to rotate in the reverse direction, and the gut was pulled

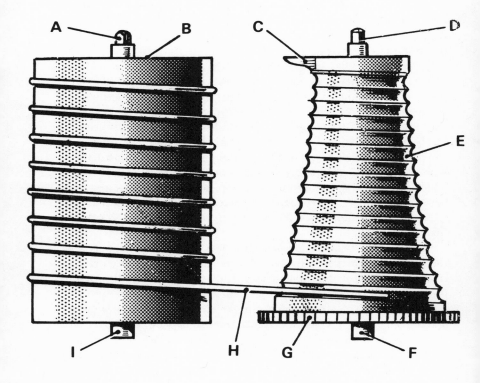

Fig. 2. Early fusee and spring barrel shown in the unwound position.

(A)	Squared end for setting up	(F)	Fusee arbor
(B)	Mainspring barrel	(G)	Great wheel
(C)	Fusee stop work arm	(H)	Gut
(D)	Squared end for winding	(I)	Mainspring barrel arbor
(E)	Fusee		

22

from the small diameter of the fusee where leverage was at its minimum. As the spring uncoiled and the barrel continued to rotate, the gut was unwound from progressively larger diameters of the fusee where leverage was proportionately greater; finally, when the spring was almost run down, the greatest diameter of the fusee was being acted upon and hence gave maximum leverage. The rotary motion of the fusee was transferred, through a pawl and ratchet, to a great wheel, mounted loosely on the fusee arbor, which drove the train of wheels.

Clockmakers found that by suitably shaping the fusee they could make the pull on its axis constant throughout the run-down of the spring. Evidence of the fusee's success is that it continues to be used, in a more sophisticated form, in present day marine chronometers.

Strangely enough, when the Nuremberg clockmakers began making watches they did not adopt the Italian method of compensation. Instead they invented a crude and much inferior device called the stackfreed, Fig. 3. The spring was not contained within a barrel. Instead, the outer end of the spring was located around a pillar held between the movement plates. The inner end of the spring was attached to the center arbor of the great wheel which transmitted the power to the wheel train. Secured to the arbor was a ratchet wheel that engaged a spring-loaded click mounted on the face of the great wheel. The end of the arbor was squared to receive a winding key; it can be seen from (a) that turning the arbor clockwise winds the spring, and on release the click holds the ratchet wheel and the assembly rotates counter-clockwise.

Secured to the great wheel center arbor was also a pinion which was geared to a stackfreed wheel, as can be seen in (b). Attached to the stackfreed wheel was a cam and pressing against its edge was a strong spring. The gear ratio between the center arbor pinion and the stackfreed wheel with cam was such that during the time taken for the mainspring to unwind fully, the cam rotated once.

The drawing at (b) shows relative positions when the mainspring is fully wound. In this condition the side pressure of the spring against the edge of the cam is at its maximum and the rate of rotation is retarded. As the spring uncoils and the cam rotates, the spring pressure is progressively reduced. The cam is so shaped that towards the end of the run-down period the side pressure of the stackfreed spring has the reverse effect; that is, it accelerates rotation and thereby maintains an equalized torque of the mainspring.

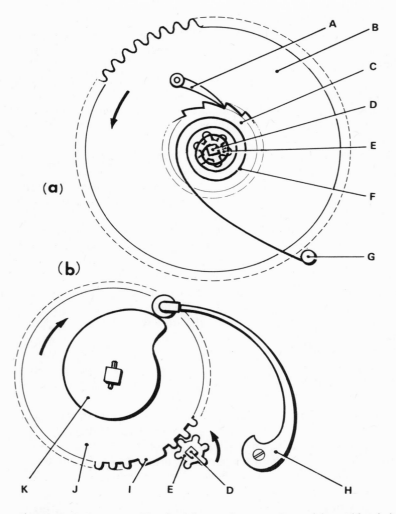

Fig. 3. Early German stackfreed in fully wound position. 1 turn of the stackfreed wheel (21 teeth) = approximately 3½ turns of great wheel = 2 plus turns of center wheel carrying hand. Most stackfreed watches run for about 26 hours. Cam revolves once during going period.

(A)	Click	(F)	Mainspring
(B)	Great wheel	(G)	Pillar between plates
(C)	Ratchet wheel	(H)	Stackfreed spring
(D)	Great wheel arbor	(I)	Stop work
	and winding square	(J)	Stackfreed wheel
(E)	Great wheel pinion	(K)	Cam

In later watches the mainspring was housed in a barrel mounted on the great wheel, and the center arbor carried the click and stop work. This is known as a going barrel.

The only advantages of a stackfreed were that it allowed a watch to run for a longer period between windings than was permitted by a fusee, usually twenty-six hours against fifteen hours of the fusee, and it allowed the plates to be positioned closer together resulting in a thinner movement. More accurate timekeeping was achieved when a fusee was used but even so the German watchmakers continued to fit the stackfreed to all their watches throughout the sixteenth century. However, by the middle of the seventeenth century its use was discontinued. The device was to be found only in Germany, whereas France, and later England, preferred the more accurate fusee.

These early watches were provided with two methods of regulation. One was to set up the mainspring when fully run down by removing the residual tension, and the other was to control the amount of swing produced by the balance.

With the early German watches, with uncased mainsprings, it was possible to wind the mainspring and remove all slackness before engaging the mainspring arbor with the stop work on the stackfreed wheel. An additional means of regulation was provided in the form of two small bristles carried on a pivoted arm. The bristles were allowed to interrupt the swing of the foliot or balance, and by moving the arm closer to or further from the center of the balance it was possible to restrict or extend the arc of swing which increased or decreased the rate of the movement accordingly.

The mainspring barrel arbor of a French or English fusee watch carried a ratchet wheel and click, and by fitting a key to the squared end of the arbor the spring could be wound and the initial set-up produced. This is known as ratchet set-up regulation. Right from the start, balances, no matter whether they were foliot or wheel, were always positioned above the top plate. The top pivot of the verge ran in a cock that was secured by being pinned to a post riveted to the top plate. The cock was spiral-shaped to allow for slight bending when adjusting the depth of engagement between the upper pallet and the escape wheel teeth. The bottom pivot of the verge ran in a spiral-shaped cock which was cut in the bottom plate and could similarly bend when adjusting the depthing of the bottom pallet.

French watches, and late sixteenth century German watches, secured the upper cock to the top plate by means of a screw. The bottom

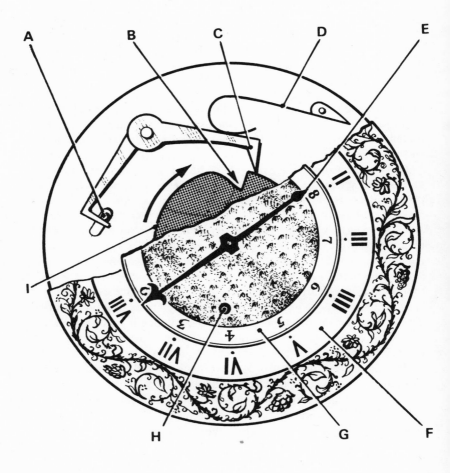

Fig. 4. Alarm mechanism. When the hand points directly at VIII, the disc I will have moved round enough to allow detent C to drop into slot B.

(A)	Alarm release pin in slot	(F)	Watch dial
(B)	Release slot	(G)	Alarm setting disc
(C)	Alarm detent	(H)	Setting hole
(D)	Light spring	(I)	Alarm release disc
(E)	Tail of hour hand		

26

pivot of the verge ran in a plain hole in the bottom plate. The escape wheel, which by the second half of t he century was much smaller in diameter, was mounted on its arbor between two pillars riveted to the top plate. At one end of the arbor the pivot ran against a push-tight plug which altered the lateral position of the arbor, thereby increasing or decreasing the depth of engagement between the escape wheel teeth and the verge pallets. This was a more satisfactory method than bending the cocks, and finer adjustments were possible.

French watches had brass wheels almost from the beginning but German movements were made entirely of iron. It was not until about 1580 that a few brass plates and, to a much lesser extent, brass wheels first appeared in Germany. Wheel trains were planted between plates separated by plain round or square pillars, one end of each riveted to the bottom plate and the other ends held to the top plate by pins. Plates were drilled and pivots ran in plain holes without oil sinks. These iron movements were without any form of decoration.

Strike or alarm mechanisms were fitted to the majority of watches and in many instances both were fitted. Those with strike mechanisms are generally known as clock-watches.

Fig. 4 illustrates the function of an alarm mechanism. The two discs G and I are fixed together and are a friction fit over the hour hand arbor which allows them to be carried round with the hour hand.

To set the alarm one inserts a blunt pointed instrument in hole H and turns the discs clockwise until the selected hour on G is opposite the hour hand tail at E.

When the arrowhead of the hour hand reaches the time at which the alarm has been set, the slot B in disc I will be opposite C and the detent will drop into the slot thereby releasing pin A and allowing the alarm train to run. An alarm mechanism has its own mainspring.

As the hour hand continues to turn, taking with it the two discs, C is lifted out of B and pin A is re-locked.

The movements of spherical watches were divided by a centrally placed horizontal plate. The strike and alarm wheel trains and the bell were in the upper half, whereas the time train operating the hour hand was in the lower.

All watches had winding keys; keyless work had not been invented.

During the first half of the century screws were not in regular use, and the few that were made had coarse and badly cut threads. The heads were dome shaped and the slots were cut in V fashion. Screws became more widely used towards the end of the century.

27

In the earliest German watches it was usual to attach the stackfreed spring to the plate by means of a screw, and the French used a screw for the click of their setting-up ratchet on fusee watches.

Cases, Dials and Hands

During the sixteenth century all watch cases were made of brass-gilt. The only forms of decoration were pierced work, usually in intricate patterns, and, on the remaining metal, engraving and fine chiselling in a variety of floral and figured designs. The function of piercing was to release the sound of the bell so that it could be heard by the wearer.

A few cases were made from soldered sheet brass but the majority were cast. The disadvantage of sheet metal was its thinness which prevented chiselling and similarly kept piercing to a minimum.

Watches and clocks had only an hour hand. It was made of iron or steel and carefully shaped, but it was also designed to be robust to withstand being turned when the wearer set the time.

The twenty-four hour system of timekeeping was in use in south-west Germany, Bohemia and Italy, and for this reason the majority of early watches were fitted with dials with twenty-four hour markings. The outer chapter ring was engraved with Roman numerals I to XII, and the inner ring carried Arabic numerals 13 to 24. The Roman numeral IIII was used instead of IV, and the Arabic figure 2 was engraved as the letter Z.

At each hour position was a small knob or touch piece, except at XII where there were two knobs. During the hours of darkness it was possible to feel the position of the hand in relation to the touch pieces and so tell the time by feel.

The dials were made of brass-gilt and the centers were decorated with engraved star-shaped patterns and floral designs.

The spherical cases were made in two halves which were held together by a hinge on one side and a catch on the other. The upper half contained the bell and was therefore pierced, and the lower half housed the time train which meant that the dial hung face downward when the watch was worn.

The drum-shaped pendant cases were about two inches in diameter and a little over half an inch deep. The bell was fitted to the back of the case, and at the front a dial protective cover and the movement were independently hinged on a common pin. The movement had to be swung out from the case for winding. The covers, backs and sides of cases were ornately pierced and delicately chiselled in heavy relief. The covers were pierced to coincide with the hour markings so that the time could be read. Pendants were drilled from front to rear so that when the pendant ring was fitted the neck cord was able to pass through from one side to the other.

By the middle of the century drum-shaped cases were being made with much reduced depth and became known as tambour cases. About 1570 the original drum shape had almost disappeared. The wide straight sides were giving way to curved narrow sides, and the hinged cover was slightly domed. Towards the end of the century decoration by chiselling became less used, preference being given to engraving.

France was slow in getting under way with her watchmaking industry and it was not until about 1590 that watches were made there in any quantity. Earlier watches had followed the German patterns but during the last decade a variety of designs appeared, the most common of which were oval and elongated octagonal with straight sides and domed covers.

Unlike German watchmakers the French confined piercing to the sides of cases and decorated covers and backs with engravings of pictorial scenes, foliage and figures.

CHAPTER 2
Novelty and Adornment
(1600-1675)

THROUGHOUT the sixteenth century watchmakers continually strived to improve the timekeeping of their movements; but, despite the high standard of workmanship, the combination of a stackfreed or fusee with a verge escapement and foliot or balance defied all their efforts at making progress, and the watches remained consistently bad timekeepers. The solution to the problem lay in future development, so, until new ideas were born and new methods invented, watchmakers devoted much of their effort to the design of cases and the appearance of their work together with the introduction of complicated work such as calendar and astronomical trains. For those collectors whose particular interest is in style and decoration the seventeenth century can possibly offer a wider variety of designs with superlative artistic craftsmanship than any other period.

From the very beginning of watchmaking Germany had always held the lead, but the Thirty Years' War (1618-1648) had such a disastrous effect on the country that France subsequently found herself in the position of supremacy, a situation that continued until 1675 when England took the lead after the invention of the balance spring.

At the beginning of the century a few watches were made in Geneva but they had no distinctive style of their own and bore a strong French influence.

Movements
The basic movement continued to have three-wheel trains and a verge escapement. Wheels and pinions were made more accurate with

improved cutting and filing, and experimentation with fusee curves produced better compensation results, but otherwise nothing was done to improve timekeeping.

Watchmakers devoted much of their time to decoration and changes of style, and variation of pattern offers a guide to when the watch was made.

Plates, wheels and other brass work continued to be gilded. More attention was given to the pillars that held the plates and they became more decorative as the century passed. (Some typical examples are illustrated in Fig. 21a on page 76.) The four most common types were the square and the round baluster, the Egyptian and the tulip, but there were many variations of each. The balusters were used throughout the sixteenth century and continued to be popular well into the seventeenth century. It was usual to fit round baluster pillars to small watches and square balusters to larger movements. About 1625 a new design appeared known as the Egyptian pillar. It was rectangular in cross-section and tapered upward and outward towards the top plate. In some of the more elaborate watches they were pierced and engraved. Then, about 1650, the tulip pillar was introduced. This was possibly the most decorative of them all.

English watches between 1605 and 1630 were invariably decorated with an engraved border round the edge of the top plate.

During the sixteenth century balance cocks took the form of a small simple spiral-shaped strip pinned to a peg riveted to the plate, but at the turn of the century they became much bigger and were decorated with fine piercing and chiselling. The area supporting the balance is known as the table, and the extension that rests on the plate is called the foot. At the junction of the table and the foot is a square hole that fits over a peg riveted to the plate. The cock is secured to the peg by a pin.

Early seventeenth century German and French balance cocks were invariably S-shaped and decorated with floral and foliage designs. English balance cocks tended to be more oval and their form of decoration was scroll work.

About 1620 watches began to appear with the cock foot held to the plate by a screw, but the cock continued to be fitted over the square peg.

By the middle of the century, when the transition period from peg to screw was over, the cocks were no longer made with a square hole and the pegs disappeared entirely. Cocks were larger and the tables had become circular and completely covered the balance. During the third quarter of the century English balance cocks were given rims to tables and feet.

From the beginning of the century pierced and engraved decorative plates were introduced to cover alarm stop work, striking trains and the click spring of a ratchet set-up. Makers' names appeared engraved on the top plates and sometimes the town in which the watch was made was included.

About 1625 the ratchet set-up regulator began to be replaced by the worm and wheel set-up, sometimes referred to as the endless screw set-up. This arrangement allowed a much finer adjustment to be made. The wheel was secured to the end of the mainspring arbor outside the top plate, and to the wheel was attached an indicator dial with engraved numbers around its edge. Usually the dial was graduated with numbers 1 to 8 but not infrequently numbers 1 to 6 or 1 to 4 were used. Secured to the plate and close to the dial was a pointer which, together with the numbers, provided a guide during regulation.

The worm was part of a long arbor which was supported at each end by a blued steel bearing. One end of the arbor was squared to receive a key. Each bearing was held to the plate by a screw and was decorated with a finely pierced tail.

During the third quarter of the seventeenth century the pierced tails of the worm arbor bearings were made larger and allowed to spread over the plate.

Until 1650 it was usual to hinge the movements to their cases so that they could be swung out for winding, but after that date winding holes with protective shutters were provided in the case backs.

About this time watchmakers began reducing the thickness of their movements by cutting away the bottom plate to make room for the balance wheel potence. Slim watches then became fashionable.

After 1660 further decoration was applied between the plates, particularly with English watches. Spring barrels were engraved and mountings for fusee stop arms were pieced.

It is known that fusee chains were introduced in a few watches early in the seventeenth century but they are very rare. It was not until shortly before 1670 that they came into common use. Occasionally a watch is found that on close inspection reveals a fusee originally made for gut but in later years altered for chain drive. The grooves of a gut-driven fusee are curved at the bottom whereas those intended for

Fig. 5a. Gilt coach watch with strike and alarm. Dial with silver chapter ring, gilt metal alarm disc and robust single hand. Case band pierced with floral design. Diameter 10.5 cm. circa 1640.

Fig. 5b. Verge movement with fusee. Pierced barrels for strike and alarm, and pierced cocks over alarm stop work and ratchet set-up. Signature J. Barberet, Paris.

chains are flat. The alteration involves cutting the grooves square at the base. The shape of the gut holes in the barrel and the fusee is the means of recognizing that this work has been carried out.

Watch and clock makers had always cut their wheels by hand. Blanks were shaped by filing and then placed centrally on a metal plate engraved with concentric guide rings and as many equally spaced radial lines as there were teeth in common use. The template indicated the positions of teeth which were then marked on the blank by an arm, pivoted at the center of the template and carrying a hardened steel point.

In 1672 Dr. Robert Hooke invented a wheel-cutting machine that allowed the blank to be rotated a pre-determined distance bringing the area between two teeth into the path of a shaped cutter. For the first time it became possible to produce wheels with uniform teeth at regular intervals on a common radius. More will be said about Hooke in Chapter Three.

Many attempts were made to improve the performance of the verge and new escapements were invented, but none were used commercially and the verge continued in its original form.

Early Seventeenth Century Watches

With little change in styling, the round, oval and elongated octagonal pendant watches of the closing years of the sixteenth century remained fashionable during the first quarter of the seventeenth century. The straight sides of cases gradually disappeared in favor of curved sides and decoration became progressively more elaborate. Piercing and chiselling were still popular, although the chiselling was more shallow than when applied during the sixteenth century and its place was slowly taken by engraving. Brass-gilt remained the most generally used metal for the manufacture of cases and dials, silver was little used at first and then gained in popularity, and enamel became general about 1630. Towards the end of the first quarter fewer oval and octagonal cases were made, and about 1625 people began wearing garments with pockets. Round watches were the fashion and these were the pre-cursors of watches that became known as pocket watches.

Form Watches

At the end of the sixteenth century Germany, France and Switzerland produced a new style that became known as the form watch. The cases were mostly engraved silver and fashioned in a variety of shapes of which some were skulls, books, crosses, birds, animals, stars and shells. They were considered as novelties and enjoyed a popularity that lasted until about 1665 after which very few were made until they reappeared in Switzerland in 1800.

Crystal Watches

From the very beginning of the seventeenth century until about 1675 rock crystal was used for making watch cases. A solid block was hollowed out to take the movement, and another piece was similarly shaped to form a cover. The mating edges of the two pieces were then fitted into brass-gilt bezels which were joined by a hinge. Clear rock crystal was almost invariably used but some watches are known to have cases made of the rare smoke-colored variety. Facets were cut in the polished crystal to provide the only form of decoration. Watches with cases of uncut crystal are very rare.

In the meantime the English watchmaking industry, centered in London and barely more than twenty years old, adopted a more serious attitude towards horology. Emphasis was placed on the development of movements that would produce an accuracy of timekeeping not previously achieved. The quality of workmanship improved and by 1625 English watches compared favorably with any made in Europe.

Puritan Watches

About 1630 England produced a plain looking watch we now refer to as the Puritan watch, probably in deference to the beliefs of those members of the Church of England who, in the time of Elizabeth and the Stuarts, rejected much of the ritual because of its strong resemblance to the Roman Catholic Church. Their aim was to extend the reformation of the Church of England by purifying it of pomp and ceremony.

The cases were silver and oval in shape with rounded sides, and almost all were without any form of decoration. The dial plates were sometimes engraved but more usually they were plain with an applied chapter ring engraved with Roman numerals. The dial covers were always fitted with a round glass window. By the middle of the century Puritan watches were very popular but little is heard of them after about 1670.

Pair-Case Watches

During the sixteenth century watch cases were made of brass-gilt with only piercing, chiselling and engraving as the means of ornamentation, but during the first three quarters of the seventeenth century frequent use was made of silver and gold, and the quality and splendor of decorative art reached a very high standard. Cases were enriched with engraved floral and foliate designs. Some portrayed figures and landscapes delicately worked in colored enamels and paints, and others were embellished with panels of onyx or tortoise-shell. Cases of strike and alarm watches continued to be pierced but the use of chiselling became less frequent in favor of fine engraving.

These highly decorative watches were vulnerable to damage from being accidentally knocked. Enamel and paint were easily cracked and chipped, and the polished surface of gold and silver became scratched if the watch was left loose in a drawer or jewelry box. The need arose for a protective case into which the watch could be placed for safety when not in use.

About 1630 pair-cases were introduced. They were made of stiff leather, or shagreen-covered silver or gold, in two halves hinged together and shaped to fit completely around the watch. The outside was decorated by tooling or by designs worked in silver or gold pins which were known as piqué work.

By the middle of the century pair-cases had become part of the watch case and the front was cut away to expose the glass and dial. The decoration of the inner case became less important and by 1670 the inner cases were usually plain.

Dials and Hands

The very early sixteenth century watches had plain dials of brass-gilt with a small engraved hour, or chapter, ring. The ring was narrow and the Roman numerals had a squat appearance, a feature that lasted until about the middle of the century. Half-hour and quarter-hour positions were marked on the ring, a fleur-de-lis being the usual symbol for the half-hours.

As watches became more decorative the area outside the chapter ring was engraved with reclining female figures and foliate designs, and the center of the dial was engraved with figures in landscape settings.

Occasionally a silver disc engraved with hour markings was applied to the dial plate instead of the more usual chapter ring.

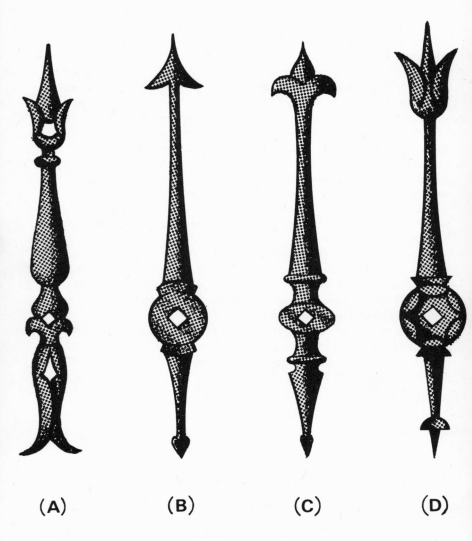

Fig. 6. 16th and 17th century single hour hands.

    (A)   German, circa 1575

    (B)   English, circa 1600; French, circa 1635

    (C)   English, circa 1620

    (D)   English, circa 1675

Alarm watches were fitted with a setting disc inside the chapter ring. The disc was usually made of pierced brass-gilt with a blued steel background, or of pierced silver over brass-gilt.

All through the seventeenth century complicated work was introduced into the movements and subsidiary dials were provided on the dial plate for calendar and astronomical readings. Silver chapter rings were fitted at apertures provided for zodiac signs, phases of the moon, and the day of the week. These multiple dials were invariably of silver and completely engraved.

During the first quarter of the seventeenth century German dials continued using the letter Z instead of the figure 2, and French dials were frequently white enamel and decorated with painted flowers.

After 1625 the hour circle carrying the Arabic numerals 13 to 24 began to disappear from German watches and applied silver chapter rings engraved with Roman numerals I to XII took their place.

From about 1650 silver and gold dials with matt surfaces became popular and the diameter of chapter rings increased. Date rings of calendar watches were fitted outside the chapter ring and were either fixed or allowed to rotate. Watches with fixed date rings had a pointer engraved on an annular ring that rotated between the date ring and the chapter ring. With a rotating date ring the day of the month corresponded with a pointer engraved on the dial plate.

Hands were robust but elegantly shaped with long tails. They were made of blued steel unless the dial was enamelled in which case the hand was gilt. During the third quarter of the century the width of chapter rings increased and hands had to be made shorter. Many of the tails disappeared altogether. Some typical examples are illustrated in Fig. 6.

Pendants

Until about 1650 pendants had a hole drilled right through from front to rear into which was fitted a loose ring; this arrangement allowed the neck cord to pass through the ring from side to side. Pendants then began to appear with a hole drilled from side to side allowing the loose-fitting ring to lie parallel to the case, possibly because such an arrangement was more suitable when the watch was suspended from a fob chain.

Watch Glasses

The first transparent dial covers to be fitted appeared about 1630.

They were circular pieces of rock crystal inserted from inside the case and held in place by metal tabs. An alternative method of securing was the use of a separate ring with two sets of tabs, the lower set bent outward to grip the case bezel, and the upper set bent inward to hold the crystal.

Plain glass windows soon followed and these were secured by either of the tab methods, or held in a split bezel, the split being made across the ring by the hinge. Cover glasses were produced by first blowing a hollow glass sphere and then cutting from it a disc of suitable size.

By 1660 snap-in bezels had appeared. These were rings with an undercut groove machined around their inner edge into which the bevel of the glass could be sprung and thereby held in place.

CHAPTER 3
Birth of the Balance Spring
(1675)

DURING the first one hundred and seventy-five years of watch history there was no development of any significance, and watches became progressively more decorative but persisted in remaining very erratic timekeepers. Watchmakers continually strove to find a means of producing a steady rate, but despite their efforts the solution remained elusive. Then, in 1675, balance wheels were fitted with a spiral spring and the immediate improvement in timekeeping was as startling as when pendulums were first fitted to clocks in 1657. The accuracy of watches was brought to within two or three minutes a day.

The man responsible for what is probably the most important contribution to the advancement of mechanical watches was Dr. Robert Hooke (1635-1703). He was a man of great intellect who rose to fame through his inborn ability to comprehend scientific subjects and to advance them with new thinking. His restless mind was forever producing new ideas, but as soon as his experiments confirmed their probability he had no patience to pursue the project before passing on to his next idea. Yet, if others extended his train of thought and successfully brought it to a practical conclusion he would hurriedly submit his claim for full acknowledgment. He was a furtive man given to much mistrust and secretiveness. Richard Waller described him as "sharp and pale of feature, crooked and lean in body, and he went stooping and fast."

At an early age Hooke became interested in the problems of designing a watch movement that would produce a good steady rate and could be regulated. He realized the solution lay in the escapement and that some means had to be found whereby the oscillations of the balance were brought under control.

In 1658 he began experimenting with springs of different shape and tension, varying their relationship with balance wheels. His idea was to employ a spring in such a way that it would immediately check and correct any irregularity in the swing of the balance. This, he believed, was the way to create a regular beat; the rest was a matter of regulation.

A number of experiments were conducted using two balance wheels geared together. In one arrangement the two pallets were carried one on each arbor. In another, both pallets were on the arbor of one wheel and the other wheel was used as a steadying influence. Different methods of regulation were tried, one of which was the use of a lodestone.

In 1668 Hooke demonstrated one of his ideas to members of the Royal Society. He used a short length of straight spring, one end fixed to the movement plate and the other end positioned centrally between two pins in the face of the balance wheel rim. When the wheel rotated, one of the pins pushed against the spring until the tension prevented further movement. The wheel stopped and the spring, in trying to regain its former shape, pushed against the pin and turned the wheel in the reverse direction beyond the central position. The cycle repeated itself and the wheel continued to oscillate.

Having convinced himself that therein lay the solution, Hooke had no further interest and he directed his inquiring brain to other scientific problems. In the meantime Christiaan Huygens had begun his own independent experiments with springs. It is possible he may have adopted the same line of reasoning as that of Hooke; at least it is known that he studied the effects of gearing together two balance wheels.

As had happened so many times before, Hooke had started something and someone else finished it, and there followed the usual explosive demands for recognition.

It was Christmas 1674 in Paris when Huygens believed he had found the solution. He had mounted a balance wheel, a spiral spring and a pinion on a common arbor, Fig. 7. The pinion was geared to a contrate wheel which was secured to the end of a verge, the pallets of which interrupted the teeth and controlled the rotation of a crown wheel. The spring had four complete turns which caused the balance wheel to rotate several times at each oscillation giving the escapement

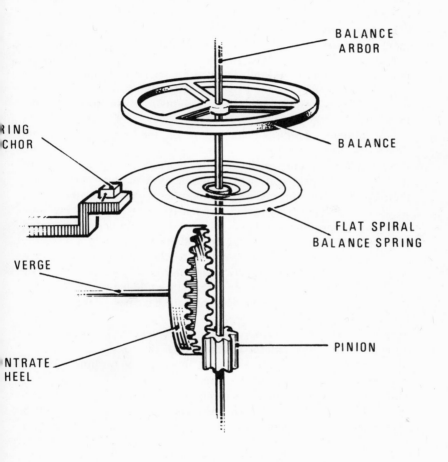

BALANCE
ARBOR

BALANCE

RING
CHOR

FLAT SPIRAL
BALANCE SPRING

VERGE

PINION

NTRATE
HEEL

Fig. 7. Christiaan Huygens' pirouette balance escapement.

43

a very slow beat. It became known as the pirouette balance spring escapement.

On January 22nd 1675 Huygens took into his confidence Isaac Thuret, one of the eminent French clockmakers of that time, and asked him to make, as quickly as possible, an escapement to his design which he could demonstrate to others. Thuret worked long hours in his workshop and within the week he completed the escapement and fitted it to a clock movement with successful results.

Huygens now wanted to begin commercial production of his invention and on January 30th he wrote to his friend in London, Henry Oldenburg, secretary to the Royal Society, giving him details of the escapement and offering him the sole rights to manufacture in England.

The following month Huygens applied to the French Academy of Science for a patent to safeguard his invention, but the Abbé Jean de Hautefeuille intervened on the grounds that he himself had previously made a similar representation to the Academy. Unknown to Huygens, the Abbé had also been engaged in experiments with escapements and had submitted the idea of using a short straight balance spring. Because legal representation was costly and carried with it no guarantee of success, Huygens decided against taking further action.

When news of Huygens' invention reached Hooke on February 17th he was filled with indignation and angrily accused Oldenburg of unethical conduct. Hooke believed that since Oldenburg had seen his demonstration at the Royal Society, he must have passed the information to Huygens.

Hooke's attack on Huygens was no less vehement. He regarded Huygens with contempt for having stolen the idea and scornfully described Huygens' design as being "not worth a farthing."

Having left no doubt of his feelings in the minds of those concerned Hooke hastened to establish his rights. He went to his friend Thomas Tompion, the man who was to become known as the father of English watch and clock makers, and asked him to make a watch using a balance spring escapement. The exact type of spring finally used is uncertain because Hooke frequently changed the design, but eventually the watch was completed. The movement was contained in a brass case, and over the balance was a pierced brass plate engraved "Rob't Hooke Iven 1658. T. Tompion fecit 1675." On April 7th Hooke, accompanied by Tompion, handed the watch to the king for his appraisal.

Charles II enjoyed anything mechanical and he was a great admirer of London's leading clock and watch makers. It is said that his bedroom was full of ticking clocks.

Hooke did not know that Oldenburg had already shown the king the watch Thuret had made for Huygens. After comparing the two watches the king showed a preference for the one designed by Hooke and asked that such a watch be made for him, implying at the same time that he would not grant the balance spring patent to Oldenburg.

Tompion had scarcely started work on the king's watch when, on April 10th, word came from the palace that in the event of any delay the king would approve the application submitted by Oldenburg. Whether or not this was calculated to ensure that the watch would be made in the quickest possible time is open to conjecture, but, be that as it may, the watch was finished and handed to the king on May 17th. Tompion had excelled himself. The movement was a great achievement and lay resplendent in a beautiful case of gold. If nothing else it most certainly brought Tompion to the notice of the king.

Not many days passed before the watch was back in Tompion's workshop in need of regulation. Hooke seized the opportunity to try out new ideas of spring application and it was not until August 26th that the watch was returned to the king.

Hooke's disposition did not allow him to acknowledge the possibility that Huygens had conducted experiments with springs without knowing something of Hooke's activities. To the despair of everyone concerned he continued to damage the reputation of Oldenburg by accusing him of deceit. Hooke claimed that Huygens had offered Oldenburg the English rights in return for information concerning his experiments, but Huygens vigorously denied this in a letter to Lord Brounckner, president of the Royal Society.

Hooke continued to experiment with different forms of springs and Tompion continued to make watches for him, but with decreasing interest. Tompion was beginning to be irritated by the restlessness of Hooke whose mind was always ahead of production.

By the end of 1675 Huygens had dispensed with his pirouette balance and had attached the balance wheel and flat spiral spring directly to the verge. It was Tompion's opinion that this arrangement was a great improvement and he began making his own watches using Huygens' latest arrangement.

Hooke's never-ending visits to Tompion with new ideas became a nuisance and Tompion began devoting less time to his demands.

Hooke became enraged at Tompion's apparent indifference and is on record as having called him "a slug," "a clownish churlish Dog" and a "Rascall," but despite this they remained friends.

Although Hooke was convinced that the use of a spring in conjunction with a balance wheel was the solution to controlled timekeeping, he was not satisfied that the best arrangement had yet been found. He continued with his experiments up to about 1679.

Tompion on the other hand felt that little improvement could be made on Huygens' arrangement, and so he settled to making watches with Huygens' escapement despite Hooke's derogatory remarks. Time proved him right. To attach a balance wheel and a flat spiral spring directly to a verge became the universally accepted arrangement.

There has been, and probably always will be, much controversy over who was responsible for introducing the balance spring. It was Tompion's opinion that the credit belonged to Hooke but at this point historical records become a little obscure.

Suffice it to say that the conclusion to all this bickering was the establishment by Tompion of a balance spring watch, and the king's refusal to grant a patent to anyone.

Footnote: The official body known as the Royal Society was founded in London in 1667 for those engaged in "the advancement of natural knowledge." Each year the Society published a volume containing details of the previous year's philosophical transactions. The title page of Volume I reads: — "Giving some Account of the Present Undertakings, Studies, and Labours of the Ingenious in many Considerable Parts of the World."

CHAPTER 4

The First Balance Spring Watches
(1675-1750)

THE invention of the spiral balance spring was a triumph of ingenuity and probably the most important step forward in development. Its effect on verge watches was quite remarkable. The gap between indifferent timekeeping and accuracy was reduced beyond expectations.

During his early years of experimenting with springs, Hooke sought the help of Tompion because of his seemingly incredible skill as a clock and watch maker. With this experience behind him Tompion was in a strong position. He was known and respected by Charles II and members of the Royal Society all of whom followed his progress with great interest. In 1675 he began making his own balance spring watches and, with the help of Hooke's wheel-cutting machine, he produced high quality watches capable of maintaining time to within a minute or two a day, an achievement never before attained. He then invented a means of regulation that allowed the effective length of the spring to be varied. Other eminent London makers such as Joseph Knibb and Daniel Quare followed his lead and their watches were unequalled in any other country.

Previously, a maker had been able to demonstrate his skill only by his application of decoration and finish. Component parts of a movement could be cut and assembled with as much precision as existing tools and equipment would allow, but the nature of the movement controller prevented accuracy in performance. Now, with the introduction of the balance spring, makers could express themselves more fully. Gone was the frustration of being without means of producing

Fig. 8.

Top left.

Gilt and leather covered oignon pendulette. Deep verge escapement movement with pierced pillars. Engraved balance cock covering almost entire top plate with pierced work for the mock pendulum bob. White enamel dial with blue Roman numerals, black minute markings and gilt beetle and poker hands. Leather covering. Signature B. Humbert à La Rochelle. Circa 1700.

Top right.

Early silver bell repeater. Large pierced and engraved balance cock. Engraved dust cover. White enamel dial with gilt filigree hands. Signature J. Zacharie. Gervais.

Bottom Left

Silver pair-case. Verge escapement. Large balance cock with streamers and large pierced foot. Tulip pillars. White enamel dial. Diameter 2¼ in. Signature T. Tompion. London. No. 424. Circa 1700.

Bottom right.

Bell repeater with verge escapement. Cast, chased and pierced silver case. Silver pillars and balance cock. White enamel dial with black and gold numerals and fancy gold hands. Diameter 1⅞ in. Signature Alelin à Miens. Circa 1740.

an accurate timekeeper. For the first time they were in a position to take as much pride in the accuracy of the instruments they made as they took in their appearance.

Simultaneously, English clocks were undergoing even greater developments and by 1680 England found herself leading the world in horology.

Clocks and watches of this period are much sought after by collectors. Fortunately a great number of both have survived, many of which are original and in excellent condition. By 1700 the period of experiments with springs was over and watchmakers in England began to standardize their work and enjoy their new-found supremacy.

Tompion's Mastery and the Size of Early Balance Spring Watches

Tompion was the acknowledged master among watch and clock makers, and when he began making balance spring watches other makers followed his example and, in many instances, his methods. He realized, probably more than anyone, the revolutionary effect the balance spring would have on the watchmaking industry. No more would watches be unreliable timepieces worn as decorative novelties by the wealthy. Hooke had shown the way to making instruments capable of much closer accuracy than ever before and further improvements would come with development. It seemed to Tompion that the demand for watches would increase rapidly and so he reorganized his workshop and administered his staff with the aim of producing and assembling components.

Tompion knew from working on Hooke's experiments that a large balance produced the best results, and he had long since found out that improved layout and performance were attainable if space was not restricted. Now that accuracy of timekeeping had become the first requirement the size of the watch was of secondary importance. The first watches of this type were bigger in diameter than earlier types. and the thickness was increased from about an inch to an inch and a quarter.

Such was Tompion's faith in the balance spring that he discarded the fusee in favor of a going barrel, but he soon realized that his optimism was premature and that with verge escapements the fusee was necessary.

Evidence that other watchmakers were closely following Tompion is reflected in their likewise discarding the fusee, not only in England but also in France. However, it is doubtful whether any balance spring verge watches were made without fusees after 1685 and those very early ones that have survived are extremely rare.

In 1682 Tompion started a system of numbering his watches, details of which are given in Chapter Nine.

The growth in size of French watches was even more considerable than English watches and it was usual for the enlarged balance to occupy the full diameter of the plate. The thickness of these watches increased to about an inch and a half and the movements were fitted in an almost spherical case suggesting the name oignon (French, "onion"). Provision for winding was usually through the dial.

Spring Balances

The flat spiral balance spring was at first untempered and soft and therefore easily distorted. The inner end passed through a round hole in the side of a brass collet that was a tight fit over the balance arbor, and the spring was held in place by a round tapered pin. The outer end passed through a round hole in the stud that was riveted to the plate or held there by a drive fit in a hole, and again a round tapered pin was used to hold the spring in position. Both Tompion and George Graham almost invariably used square holes and square pins.

The first balance springs were made with one and a half turns, but by 1750 the length had increased and it was then more usual for a spring to have between four and five turns.

With any balance spring it is essential to ensure that the effective length, i.e. the length from the regulator to the arbor collet, be allowed to expand and contract without physical contact with any part of the watch. Any such contact momentarily reduces the effective length and the watch gains.

Balances were made of polished steel with three arms. Where the rims of very large balances extended beyond the winding square, two of the arms were cranked to make room for the key.

Balance Cocks

Shortly after balance spring watches were introduced in 1675, English brass-gilt balance cocks underwent a series of changes in decoration, shape and size. These changes provide a useful guide to the age of a watch within the period covered by this chapter.

Prior to 1675, tables, i.e. that part of the cock above the balance, and feet were decorated with pierced work in floriate and foliate patterns, and their profiles were irregular. The size of many tables barely covered the balance wheel and on such watches the rim of the balance is clearly visible.

The very early balance spring watches had quite large balances. Cock tables were made circular but rimless, and large enough to cover the balances completely. Some of these tables were almost as large as the movement plate. They retained the pierced work as their form of decoration, but the pre-balance foliate and floriate designs gave way to more open and flowing forms of arabesque patterns that were further enhanced with heavy engraving and light chiselling. These arabesque patterns were symmetrical about a line drawn through the center of the table and its foot.

The profile of cock feet assumed a more irregular shape than hitherto but they were decorated with the more fashionable arabesque pierced work.

From 1675 to about 1695 a few watchmakers continued to decorate balance cocks with foliate and floriate pierced work but it became increasingly perfunctory. The surfaces were quite flat with shallow engraving, and the frets were very close producing an uninteresting appearance.

About 1680 the arabesque pattern in the table emanated from a mask in the form of a woman's head or a shell at the point where the table met the foot. These masks were small at first, becoming larger by 1685. They remained with English verge watches until about 1850.

By 1685 the irregular outlines of both table and foot had almost disappeared and had been replaced by definite rims, that of the table being completely round and that of the foot opening out and extending to the edge of the movement plate. During the next few years the pierced work spread until, about 1695, it almost completely covered the plate leaving just enough space near the edge for the maker's signature. The arabesque designs then became closer and less defined, and the chiselling and engraving disappeared. At the end of the seventeenth century, watchmakers further ornamented the mask at the top of the foot by adding a streamer at each side.

The design of balance cocks then became standardized throughout the first quarter of the eighteenth century and it was not until a little after 1725 that the next change in style occurred. Pierced work on feet had by this time become uninteresting and devoid of character, and the beginning of the second quarter of the century saw the introduction of the solid foot decorated with simple engraved designs.

About 1730 the original bold arabesque designs with flowing curves, worked in chiselled frets, returned to fashion in English provincial areas and again decorated balance cock tables until about 1780. In the meantime London makers introduced the rococo style of decoration to their tables. This new fashion appeared about 1740 and the designs were almost always assymmetrical.

During this period, French and Swiss watchmakers paid far less attention to decorating their top plates than did their English counterparts. Other than the balance cock, little else received any form of ornamentation. The cocks were made in the form of a large bridge held to the plate by a screw at each side, and they completely covered the balance wheel. Some tables were decorated with pierced and chiselled designs similar in style to rococo work, and others were solid, painted with enamel or engraved.

A highly polished steel plate, shaped like a keyhole, was screwed to the table, and the circular end was used as an end bearing for the balance top pivot and was known as a coqueret.

About 1740 some French and Swiss watches had cocks made of silver, whereas others were decorated with enamel and made visible through a small window in the back of the case.

The chart provides a quick reference.

BALANCE COCKS

DATE	FEATURE
1675	Profile of tables was circular, and that of feet was irregular. Both were without rims.
1675-1695	Arabesque patterns in use. Some watches retained the foliate and floriate designs but they had deteriorated.
1675-1740	Table patterns remained symmetrical.
1680-1850	Masks were in use. Small at first, bigger by 1685.
1685	Table and foot had rims. Foot spread to edge of plate.
1695	Fret spread and almost covered plate. Arabesque designs became close and uninteresting.
1700	Masks decorated with streamers.

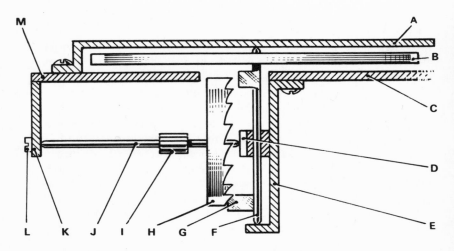

Fig. 9. Adjustable potence.

(A)	Balance cock	(H)	Crown escape wheel
(B)	Balance	(I)	Crown wheel pinion
(C)	Top plate	(J)	Crown wheel arbor
(D)	Sliding plate for lateral	(K)	Potence
	adjustment of crown wheel	(L)	Adjusting screw for
(E)	Potence		depthing crown wheel
(F)	Verge or balance arbor	(M)	Top plate
(G)	Pallet		

1725   Introduction of solid foot.

1730-1780   Original arabesque style fashionable in provinces.

1740   Assymmetrical rococo patterns introduced in tables.

Adjustable Potence

In a verge watch the bearing for the lower pivot of the verge or
balance arbor was held in a potence which was secured to the under-
side of the top plate. An arm from the potence carried the pivot
bearing for the inner end of the crown escape wheel arbor, and a

second potence, secured at the edge of the top plate, carried the pivot bearing for the outer end of the crown escape wheel arbor.

The position of a crown escape wheel in relation to the pallets of its verge was critical and about 1725 Julien Le Roy, the leading French horologist in his time, invented the adjustable potence, Fig. 9. He arranged for the inner bearing to be carried in a sliding plate held to the arm of the potence by a screw. When the screw was slackened and the plate moved to a new position, the crown escape wheel was moved laterally across the pallets and the beat of the watch was altered.

At the same time, Le Roy fitted a screw adjustment to the outer potence. Turning the screw either increased or decreased the depthing of the crown escape wheel with the pallets and thereby altered the arc of swing of the balance.

This invention dispensed with the need to disassemble a movement when adjusting the escapement and from about 1730 it was in regular use among French watchmakers. Even so, it is rarely seen in English watches.

Regulators

A pendulum clock was regulated by altering the effective length of its pendulum. This was done by raising or lowering the pendulum weight. Lowering the weight increased the effective length and slowed the rate of the clock, whereas raising the weight decreased the length and speeded up the rate. So it was with a balance spring watch and Tompion lost little time in designing a regulator for his watches that would vary the effective length of the balance spring according to requirements.

Tompion's arrangement, Fig. 10, consisted of a toothed segment positioned directly beneath the balance spring and concentric with the balance arbor. It had a radius the same as that of the outer coil of the spring. At one end of the segment were two small steel pins set apart just enough to allow the outer coil to pass between them freely. The segment was geared to a small wheel mounted on a square-ended arbor. Secured to the upper face of the geared wheel was a polished steel plate around the edge of which were engraved the numbers 1, 2, 3, 4, 5, 6 or 5, 10, 15, 20, 25. The balance was covered by a pierced fret, part of which acted as a pointer for the ring of numbers. A key was placed over the square and when the geared wheel was turned so that the numbers passing the pointer increased in value, the segment carried the pins closer to the inner end of the spring thus reducing its

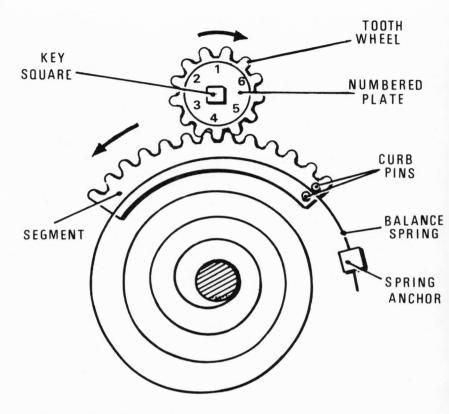

Fig. 10. Tompion's balance spring regulator.

effective length and making the watch go faster. The reverse was the case when the geared wheel was turned in the opposite direction.

In the very early days of balance spring watches Nathaniel Barrow designed a regulator called a worm and slide, that was less sophisticated than Tompion's but employed the same principle of altering the effective length of the spring. A long square-ended continuous screw, carrying a threaded slide, was mounted on the top plate between two brackets. The outer coil of the spring passed between two pins in the slide, and when the continuous screw was turned by a key the slide moved along the screw and along the outer coil thus altering the effective length of the spring. Unlike Tompion's arrangement where the two pins moved in an arc, the slide on Barrow's regulator moved in a straight line which meant that the end of the outer coil of the spring had to be straight. This arrangement was thus unnecessarily large and required considerably more space on the top plate than was needed by Tompion's regulator. It was therefore little used and surviving watches with this type of regulator are very rare.

The superior arrangement of Tompion's regulator was universally adopted and was used during the remaining years of the seventeenth century and throughout the eighteenth century. European watchmakers introduced one alteration to their watches by fixing the regulator dial plate and attaching an indicating hand to the squared end of the arbor.

Verge watches were very responsive to balance spring regulators and a movement that required more than slight adjustment to correct its rating was, almost without exception, going to be troublesome.

On the first few balance spring watches that Tompion made he continued to fit the mainspring set-up regulator on the top plate, but he soon realized that his balance spring regulator made the set-up regulator superfluous. It was accordingly moved to a position between the plates for use by watchmakers when assembling movements either during manufacture or after disassembly for cleaning or repair.

In the majority of French watches, and late eighteenth century and early nineteenth century English watches, the set-up was fitted between the dial and the bottom plate. English watches made after that time had their set-up regulators fitted beneath the top plate.

Verge Escapement

During the first twenty years after the introduction of the balance spring, the verge continued in general use unchallenged by any other form of escapement. The combined effect of the balance spring, machined wheel cutting, and better quality mainsprings, was a more accurate rating. The improved performance obtained from these stages of development encouraged watchmakers to experiment further with the verge and they found that by increasing the angle formed by the pallets to approximately one hundred degrees a closer rate was possible. The verge defied all further attempts at improvement and continued in use for another two hundred years despite the numerous and more sophisticated escapements that were invented meanwhile.

Fig. 11a. Silver repousse pair-case verge escapement watch. The silver champleve dial has an arcaded minute ring and was probably made for the Dutch market. Calendar aperture beneath dial center. Diameter 2¼ in. Signed L. Moore. London. No. 1206. Circa 1730.

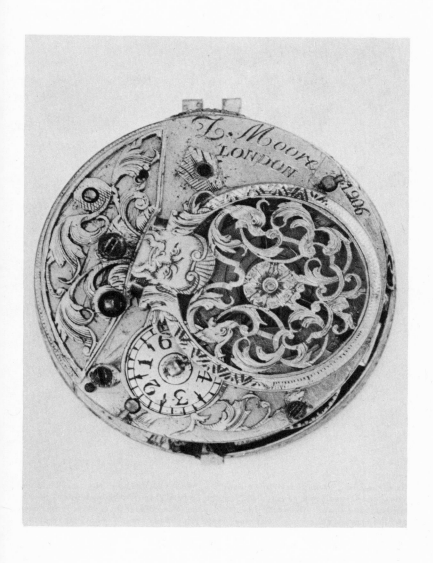

Fig. 11b. Top plate view of movement.

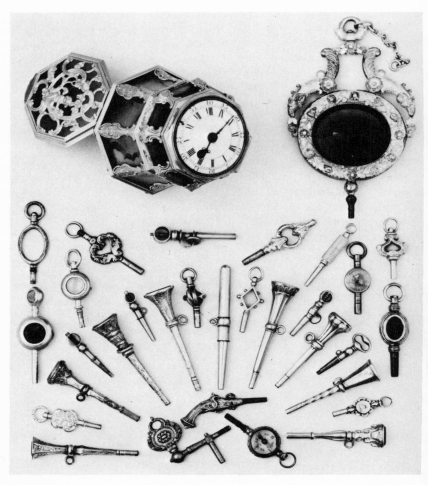

Fig. 12.

Top left.

Gold-mounted grey agate snuff box with watch. The snuff compartment has a scroll pilaster frame and hinged cover mounted with rococo and floral scrollwork enclosing a cherub seated upon a branch. The watch is mounted in the ogee base. It has a verge escapement and the enamel dial carries blued steel hands. The movement is signed Thos. Broome, London, 2022. Circa 1770.

Top right.

Multi-colored gold and amethyst watch key. The swivel frame is cast with flowers on a matted ground and is set with a large facetted amethyst. Swiss. Circa 1840.

Bottom.

An assortment of 18th and 19th century watch keys.

A first class verge watch was capable of an accuracy to within a minute a day, although even this was liable to fluctuation with varying conditions. Watchmakers were very aware that although the introduction of the balance spring left the way open to precision timekeeping, this could never be achieved with a verge escapement.

Cylinder Escapement

The first serious rival to the verge escapement came at the end of the seventeenth century when Tompion, with the help of Edward Barlow and William Houghton, invented the cylinder escapement. The idea was covered by a patent in 1695 but it is believed that little effort was made to manufacture it commercially. Certainly no known watch by Tompion with this type of escapement fitted has survived, and so it seems the idea was shelved until late in the first quarter of the eighteenth century when George Graham began taking an interest in the cylinder.

It was Graham who introduced the dead beat escapement to clocks after the introduction of the pendulum, and now he was to perform a similar service for watches by taking up the development of the cylinder where Tompion had left it. By 1725 Graham had so improved the performance of the cylinder that from 1727 he used it in all his own watches.

The principle of operation can be seen in Fig. 13. The balance and spring are mounted on the upper end of the cylinder which is provided with an upper and lower pivot.

When a tooth of the escape wheel is trapped inside the cylinder, the escape wheel is at rest, as at A. If the balance swings counter clockwise, viewed from above, the tooth is released, as shown at B, and the curved face of the tooth gives the cylinder an impulse as it escapes. The succeeding tooth advances and is arrested by the outside of the cylinder, as at C. The balance completes its swing and then changes direction, as at D, until the nose of the second tooth enters the cylinder, as at E, and the cylinder receives a second impulse, this time in the reverse direction. The tooth passes into the cylinder, as at F, and again the escape wheel is at rest. The balance continues its swing, as at G, and then reverses its direction, as at A, before carrying on to repeat the cycle.

The cylinder prevents any recoil of the escape wheel and it is therefore a dead beat escapement. Its predecessor, the verge, was fitted vertically in the movement, and because the escape wheel of the

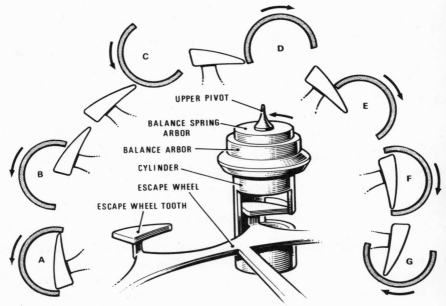

Fig. 13. Cylinder escapement.

cylinder escapement was fitted horizontally it was frequently referred to as the horizontal escapement, a term that has long since fallen into disuse.

In 1727, Le Roy visited Graham and asked to see the cylinder escapement. He was so impressed with the design that he followed Graham's example and used it in his own watches. Whether or not the adoption by these two famous watchmakers was the reason for the subsequent popularity of the cylinder is difficult to say, but there is no doubt that it became widely used and continued to be very popular during the following one hundred and fifty years.

Even so, the cylinder escapement had its disadvantages. It was considerably less robust than the verge and took much longer to make. In the hands of a skilled man it took at least three days to produce an escape wheel. It was fragile and very prone to damage from shock and handling. For these reasons the popularity of the verge continued despite the increasing use of the cylinder.

The original escape wheels were made of brass and the cylinders of steel. It was discovered that the brass teeth had an abrasive effect causing rapid wear to the entry and exit faces of the cylinder. One attempt to overcome this problem was to arrange the escape wheel teeth in three tiers to distribute the wear over a greater area, but more effective was the introduction of steel escape wheels about the middle of the eighteenth century.

Many early wheels were made with ten or twelve teeth, but Graham used thirteen and in subsequent years fifteen became more usual.

About 1764 cylinders made of ruby were introduced, but they were little used until Abraham-Louis Breguet adopted the idea and made them popular.

Watchmakers found that a cylinder escapement would function better if fitted with a balance smaller than was customary with a verge. This enabled smaller cock tables to be used thereby effecting a reduction in the size of movements.

Energy from the mainspring had less influence over the balance than was the case with a verge, and the balance swung with greater freedom of motion. For this reason the fusee fell into disuse among French and Swiss watchmakers and they were therefore able to make further reductions in the size of their movements. English watchmakers were less optimistic and they continued to fit the fusee.

Watchmakers agreed that the cylinder escapement produced an improved rating over the verge, but it had also shown that it was incapable of complete accuracy. The attainment of precise timekeeping was the ultimate aim and so development continued in the search for the ideal controller.

Debaufre Escapement

In 1704 Peter Debaufre designed the first of the frictional rest escapements. Two identical escape wheels, with teeth shaped like those of a circular saw, were mounted near one another on a horizontal arbor. The wheels were positioned so that their teeth were staggered equidistantly.

Between the two sets of teeth was the vertical balance arbor carrying a single pallet that interrupted the passage of the teeth. Because of the shape of the pallet it is sometimes referred to as the club-foot verge.

In Fig. 14 a tooth of the twin escape wheel C2 has been arrested by the pallet locking face and the escape wheel is at rest. The balance is rotating in a clockwise direction and when the pallet moves clear of the tooth, the tooth slips past the locking face G and exerts a force on

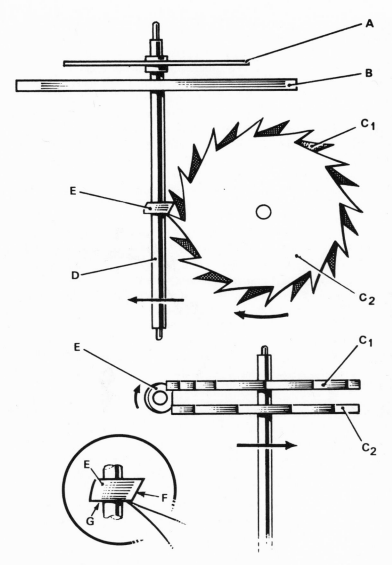

Fig. 14. Debaufre escapement.

(A)	Balance spring	(D)	Balance arbor
(B)	Balance	(E)	Pallet
(C1)	Escape wheel	(F)	Pallet impulse face
(C2)	Escape wheel	(G)	Pallet locking face

the angular face F giving an impulse to the balance. The tooth then escapes from the influence of the pallet and the escape wheel rotates.

In the meantime the balance has continued to rotate bringing the locking face of the pallet into the path of the oncoming tooth of twin wheel C1. Again the escape wheel is brought to rest until the balance completes its swing and changes direction. The cycle is then repeated. This arrangement produces an impulse for each swing of the balance.

The Debaufre escapement was not popular during the eighteenth century and of the few watches that were so fitted, none, so far as is known, have survived. However, in 1800 there was a revival of this escapement. Large numbers were produced by makers living in the town of Ormskirk, near Liverpool, England, and it became known as the Ormskirk escapement.

Rack Lever Escapement

The rack lever escapement, Fig. 15, was invented in 1722 by the Abbé de Hautefeuille. It is a development of the dead beat escape-

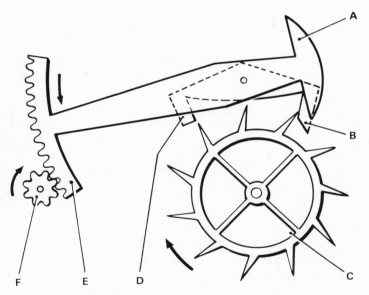

Fig. 15. Rack lever escapement.

(A)	Anchor	(D)	Entry pallet
(B)	Exit pallet	(E)	Rack
(C)	Escape wheel	(F)	Pinion on balance arbor

ment, invented by Graham in 1715, for use in clocks.

In the illustration one of the teeth has been arrested by the locking face of the exit pallet and the escape wheel is held stationary. The anchor rocks in a counter clockwise direction and when the locking face of pallet B moves clear of the tooth, the tooth escapes and exerts a force on the impulse face of the pallet.

In the meantime pallet D has dropped and arrested the oncoming tooth thus preventing further rotation of the escape wheel.

At the completion of its swing the balance moves in the reverse direction. Pallet D is raised and the tooth is released. The escape wheel turns until pallet B arrests the leading tooth thus completing the cycle. It can be seen that impulse is given to each alternate swing of the balance.

The anchor moves through an arc of about ten degrees but a much greater swing is required by a balance before it will function. This is achieved by the rack and pinion whose gear ratio imparts a swing to the balance of about two revolutions.

This escapement was never popular during the eighteenth century, but in 1791 a similar escapement, employing the same principles of operation, was invented and patented by Peter Litherland of Liverpool.

In Lancashire, England, during the early years of the nineteenth century, large numbers of watches were made with this escapement.

Repeaters

Clock-watches were among the first watches ever to be made. Their strike was controlled by a locking plate just as mediaeval clocks had been before them. This arrangement continued for a further century and three-quarters until, in 1676, Edward Barlow invented a new method of control known as rack striking.

This new method made possible the introduction of repeating work and it was not long before Barlow and Tompion were working together fitting rack striking and repeat mechanisms to clocks. The arrangement gained in popularity because it became possible to find out the approximate time in the dark without the laborious process of producing a light. Barlow then worked on a design suitable for use in watches and in 1685 he asked Tompion to make a watch incorporating the invention.

The operation was effected by two small pins, or push-pieces, one on either side of the pendant. Depressing one pin caused the watch to

Fig. 16. Repoussé and pierced gold repeater. Gold and enamel dial with blued steel hands. Shagreen pair-case. Diameter 5.8 cm. Signature F. Gaudin à Nyon. Circa 1680.

Fig. 17a. Strike and alarm carriage clock. Pierced silver case. Restored by Jos. William-son. London. Diameter 11.5 cm. Signature Laudrean. Bordeaux. Circa 1680.

Fig. 17b. Top plate view of movement.

strike the hour on one bell, whereas the other pin released a double strike on two bells of different tone for each quarter. This was known as a quarter repeater or a ting-tang quarter.

During the period of Barlow's experimenting Daniel Quare had been working on the same idea and he produced a repeating watch at about the same time but with a difference. Whereas Barlow's watch required two pins, each with its own action, Quare's was designed to operate from one pin only. Both men applied for a patent and the two watches were submitted to Charles II for his judgement. The king finally chose Quare's idea as the best and he was granted a patent in 1687.

Almost as soon as Quare went into production he changed the design so that the pendant could be depressed to operate the repeat mechanism thereby dispensing with the need for a separate push-piece. The first of such watches developed a fault in that the incorrect hour was struck if the pendant was not pressed fully home. The trouble was overcome by fitting an all-or-nothing piece which prevented any striking until the pendant was fully depressed.

It was not long before a further development was introduced. In addition to the single blows for each hour and the double blows for each quarter, a single blow was made on the second bell if seven and a half minutes, or more, had elapsed since the beginning of the quarter. This was known as the half quarter repeater.

About 1710 the five-minute repeater appeared. This arrangement allowed the hour to be struck in the usual way, and then one blow was made on the second bell for every subsequent five minutes up to the numeral eleven. Very few of these watches were made before 1750.

The bells of all these watches were fitted in the back of the case and were shaped to envelop the movement rather like a protective cover. The sound of the hammer striking the bell was usually rather loud and often the cause of embarassment to the owner. This was overcome about 1715 by fitting what was called a pulse-piece or deaf-piece. It was a means of preventing the hammers from striking the bell by restricting their travel. The owner actuated the mechanism by moving a small pin that projected from the edge of the case, and felt, rather than heard, the hammer blows.

In the second quarter of the century dust covers for movements began to appear, and in 1730 Graham dispensed with the use of bells in his repeater watches and arranged for the hammers to strike the cover.

About the middle of the century, Le Roy followed Graham's example and dispensed with bells. In their place he fitted wire gongs, an arrangement that subsequently assisted in the production of slimmer watches.

Le Roy also fitted some of his repeaters with a metal block instead of wire gongs. These are known as dumb repeaters.

A repeat mechanism had its own train of wheels and governor, and was powered by its own mainspring. The action of selecting repeat wound up the spring which powered the train and operated the hammers. A typical example of hour striking repeat work is shown in Fig. 18.

When pendant plunger A is depressed it swings push-piece B about its pivot C and at the same time causes the hour rack G to rotate. In rotating, the saw-like teeth, on the periphery of the hour rack, click past the hour hammer pallet H with an action like that of a pawl and ratchet.

The hour rack is mounted on the square-ended arbor of the repeat train mainwheel which also carries the spiral spring that drives the repeat mechanism. Turning the hour rack winds the spring; this winding continues until the nose of push-piece B is arrested by one of

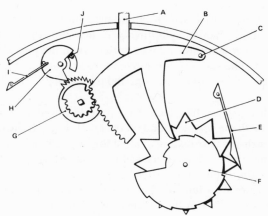

Fig. 18. Hour striking repeat work.

(A)	Pendant plunger	(F)	Hour snail
(B)	Push-piece	(G)	Hour rack
(C)	Pivot	(H)	Hour hammer pallet
(D)	Star wheel	(I)	Light spring
(E)	Jumper spring	(J)	Hammer pin

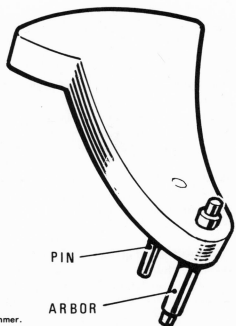

Fig. 19. Strike hammer.

PIN

ARBOR

the lands of hour snail F which is mounted on star wheel D. In the earliest repeat mechanism winding was accomplished by a chain which passed over a pulley and was pulled when the pendant plunger was depressed. The star wheel is moved forward once an hour by a pin on the quarter rack or cannon pinion, and is held in position by jumper spring E.

The number of saw-like teeth that pass the hour hammer pallet corresponds with the selected land on the snail. Fig. 18 shows that the nose of the push-piece is resting against the 10 o'clock land and at the same time that ten teeth have passed the hour hammer pallet; since only two remain to pass the pallet.

When pressure on plunger A is released, the repeat mainspring rotates the hour rack G in the reverse direction, and as the saw-like teeth run forward each one trips the pallet thus causing the hammer to strike the bell.

A typical hammer is shown in Fig. 19. The arbor is mounted between plates and the pin projects through a slot and is struck by the rotating hour hammer pallet H.

Trains

Before the introduction of the balance spring almost all verge watches had a train of three wheels with a running period of fifteen hours, but when balance spring watches were introduced it was found that they needed less power to drive them than had hitherto been required. The mainsprings were too powerful and the movements ran too fast.

Among the very first balance spring watches with three-wheel trains were a few with fusees that had an unusually large number of turns, as many as seventeen in some instances, and pinions with five leaves. They had a running period of twenty-six hours but they were far from smooth in action.

Watchmakers overcame this power problem by using four-wheel trains with six-leaf pinions. This arrangement provided smooth running as well as a twenty-six hour going period and was universally accepted.

The introduction of minute hands had an effect on the trains. It became necessary to rearrange the wheels so that the second wheel, rotating once an hour, took up a new position in the center to drive the minute hand.

Jewelled Pivot Holes and Oil Sinks

Some of the power in the mainspring of a watch was consumed in overcoming frictional resistance set up by moving parts. This was particularly so between interlocking leaves and teeth of pinions and wheels. These could not be lubricated because the oil thickened from the addition of dust and subsequent oxidization left a sticky deposit.

The same problem applied to the bearing surface between pivots and pivot holes but to a much lesser extent and so these areas of friction were lubricated. The difficulty proved to be in retaining the oil in the hole because the oil, attracted by the surface of the plate, spread, leaving the pivot without oil. The round pivot holes became elongated, and microscopic particles of steel dust from the pivots embedded themselves in the soft brass creating an abrasive and wearing the pivots. Much harder pivot holes were needed and in 1704 the problem was solved.

Living in London at that time was a Swiss, Nicholas Facio de Duillier, and the Frenchman Debaufre and between them they discovered a method of cutting and piercing precious stones. They applied for a patent to cover "An Art of Working Pretious or more

Common Stones (whether Naturall or Artificial), Christal or Glass, and certain other Matters different from Metals, so that they may be employed and made use of in Clockwork or Watchwork and many other Engins, not Ornament only, but as an Internal and useful for part of the work or Engine itselfe, in such Manners as have not heretofore been used, and that the said Art will be very beneficial to the Trade of Makeing Watches and Clocks.''

The patent was granted, but, unfortunately for them, when the time came for the patent to be extended Parliament rejected the request because of strong opposition from the Company of Clockmakers, and watchmakers and jewellers. The English did however keep the knowledge to themselves and the art of jewelling remained a secret for almost a century.

The first jewels to be used were large diamond endstones in balance cocks for the upper pivots of balance arbors in top quality watches. Their use was rare before 1715 but they became more usual by 1750.

The problem of oil starvation in pivot holes because of surface attraction was overcome in 1715 by an Englishman, Henry Sully, who at that time was living in France. He and Le Roy discovered that a film of oil spreading over a flat surface was reluctant to turn sharp corners or edges, and so they machined a bowl-shaped recess around the pivot hole and found that this arrangement held the oil and prevented creeping. These recesses became known as oil sinks. It is surprising that, despite the obvious advantages, they were rarely used before 1750.

Pillars

The design of plate pillars used during the sixteenth and early seventeenth centuries continued, but many new ones were introduced and, like the earlier patterns, they reflected a strong architectural influence until about 1745 when new designs took on a more ornate appearance. Figs. 21a and 21b illustrate the most popular basic types but many watchmakers made changes in detail to create individuality; consequently there were many variations of each.

The Egyptian pillar (e) was frequently decorated with engraving, and the square tapered pillar (f) was more often plain. The Dutch pillar (g) had a comparatively short life but strangely enough it reappeared very occasionally in watches of a much later date. It was essentially a Dutch design although it has been known to appear in English watches.

Fig. 20. Carriage clock. Jewelled movement with fusee and chain. Strikes hours and quarters. Alarm mechanism. Silver case and shagreen pair-case. White enamel dial with gilt alarm disc. Diameter 11.6 cm. Signature Antony Badl. Augsburg. Circa 1745.

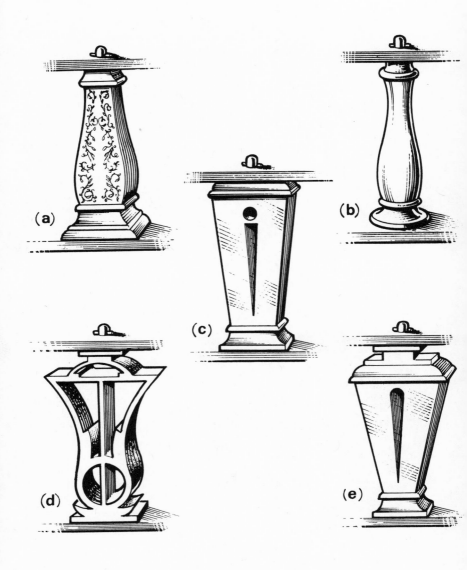

Fig. 21a. Movement plate pillars.
(a)   Square baluster (large movements), 1500-circa 1680
(b)   Round baluster (small movements), 1500-circa 1680
(c)   Narrow Egyptian, circa 1625
(d)   Tulip, circa 1650
(e)   Broad Egyptian, circa 1700

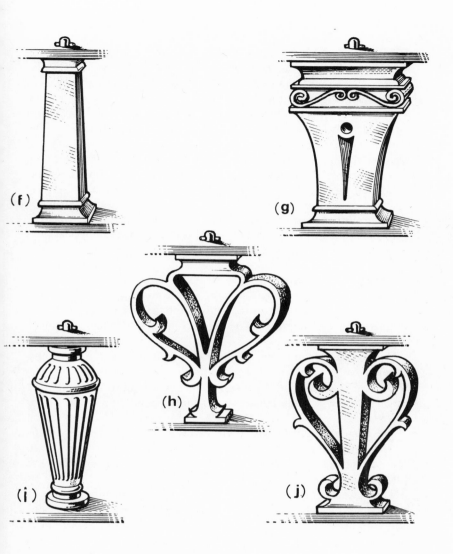

Fig. 21b. Movement plate pillars

 (f) Square tapered, circa 1730-circa 1810

 (g) Dutch verge occasionally. English sometimes. Also used much later. Circa 1730-circa 1770.

 (h) English, circa 1745.

 (i) French and German. Rarely English. Frequently silver. Circa 1750.

 (j) Dutch, circa 1750.

Pillar (h) was the forerunner of the ornate pillars and is reminiscent of English tastes of that period. Pillar (i) was predominantly used in French and German watches and was frequently made of silver. Pillar (j) was used almost exclusively by Dutch watchmakers and appears to be an acknowledgment of English fashion.

The movements of clock-watches and repeaters were of necessity rather large because of the space taken up by the mechanisms. To prevent further aggravation of this problem plain round pillars that required the minimum of space were used. The pillars were made with a flange at each end to provide good bearing surfaces with the plates.

In their oignon watches the French almost invariably used the Egyptian type of pillar but later changed to the round baluster when they introduced their thin movements that were not hinged to cases.

From about 1710 French and Swiss watches began to appear with silver cocks and these watches almost invariably had silver pillars.

Pendulum Watches

The pendulum watch was no more than a novelty. A small disc of metal was attached to one of the arms of the balance which was made visible through an aperture. The oscillations of the balance produced the illusion of a pendulum.

Dutch, French and Swiss watches with their bridge cocks completely covering the balance were well suited to this arrangement. The cock table was made solid with no pierced work, and an aperture was cut, through which the apparently swinging pendulum could be observed.

The English cock with its single foot was not so convincing. Thus the majority of English pendulum watches had the balance fitted between the bottom plate and the dial, through which an aperture was cut to make the pendulum visible.

These watches first appeared shortly after the introduction of the balance spring but, apart from Holland where their popularity continued to about 1740, very few were made after about 1710.

Cases

With the introduction of the balance spring and the resultant improvement in performance, watches were no longer pieces of novelty adornment to be worn around the neck; rather they had become instruments capable of more serious attempts at measuring time. The first of these watches, tending to be bulky and somewhat heavy, might

Fig. 22a. Copper and enamel case signed by Les frères Huaut. Enamel landscape painting on inside of cover. Enamel dial with Roman and Arabic numerals. Diameter 4.8 cm. Circa 1720.

Fig. 22b. Ornately decorated movement with silver and rock crystal balance cock. Note the plate pillars. Signature Markwick, London.

have presented a problem but for the arrival of the long waistcoat introduced to English fashion about 1675 by Charles II. From then on it became usual to wear watches in the pocket.

The oval and octagonal shapes, so popular in the early part of the sixteenth century, quickly disappeared and the more practical round cases became the fashion.

The high quality of decoration that had been maintained during the first three quarters of the seventeenth century continued only until the end of the century and then there was a marked decline. After about 1725 the exquisite artistry of seventeenth century case decoration became increasingly rare.

About 1670 repoussé began replacing cast and chiselled work, and by the end of the century it was the most common form of decoration for outer cases. The quality of repoussé work was at its highest during the second quarter of the eighteenth century and many exquisite examples of scenes and groups of figures have survived. The depth of relief in some of this work was so great that the embosser had to solder together two sheets of metal.

At the same time the quality of engraving began to deteriorate into a shallow pretense of the engravers' skill of earlier years. Eventually it almost disappeared. The little engraving that was done was generally confined to repeaters and clock-watches.

Filigree work was not unknown but it was rare and was used only during the last quarter of the seventeenth century.

Up to about 1715 skins from various sources were used on outer cases but after that time almost invariably only genuine shagreen was used.

There is an abundance of French and Swiss watches from this period with cases decorated with painting on enamel, many of which have survived with remarkably little damage. They are always popular among collectors.

The most common type of English watch was undoubtedly the pair-case. It was made of 22 carat gold, silver or gilt, and was quite plain. The owner wound the watch through a hole in the inner case.

It became the practice for makers to stamp their cases with their initials and on high quality work the movement number was included.

Case hinges were square at the ends until about 1695 and then cases began to appear with hinges chamfered or rounded at the ends.

The French counterpart of the English pair-case watch was the oignon. It was about an inch and a half thick, and bulbous in shape. Of those that have survived almost all have gilt or silver pair-cases; gold is extremely rare. The gilt inner cases are usually cast with a design that has been finished by chiselling, and the outer cases are frequently made of leather. The most common French case during the last quarter of the seventeenth century was a single gilt case that was completely covered by pierced arabesque designs.

Glasses with snap-in bezels first appeared about 1660 but the original method of holding a glass by the split bezel method continued in use until about 1705.

Pierced cases encouraged the admission of dirt into the movement and about 1710 gilt dust caps were introduced, probably by Graham, which allowed regulation and winding without their removal. Their popularity grew and by 1725 they were in common use.

About 1720, a London clock and watch maker, Christopher Pinchbeck, introduced an alloy of four parts copper and three parts zinc and produced a metal remarkably like gold in appearance. This new metal was named after its inventor and became widely used for the less expensive watch cases.

Dials

The greatly improved rating made possible by the introduction of the balance spring decided English watchmakers that some means of indicating minutes was now justifiable. Among the many methods tried, the most practical were the following:

1. the addition of a minute hand placed concentrically with the hour hand, and the inclusion of a minute ring on the dial, circa 1678
2. the wandering hour dial, circa 1680
3. the sun and moon dial, circa 1685
4. the six hour dial, circa 1685
5. the differential dial, circa 1700

As we all know, the use of two hands became the accepted method.

The Minute Hand

The addition of a minute hand necessitated re-designing the dials, Fig. 23. With the single hour hand the chapter ring was wide and it extended to the watch glass bezel ring. When the minute hand was added, the diameter and width of the chapter ring had to be reduced to make room for a minute ring and minute numerals. Roman figures continued to be used for the chapters, and Arabic figures were placed outside the minute ring to indicate minutes, usually at five-minute intervals.

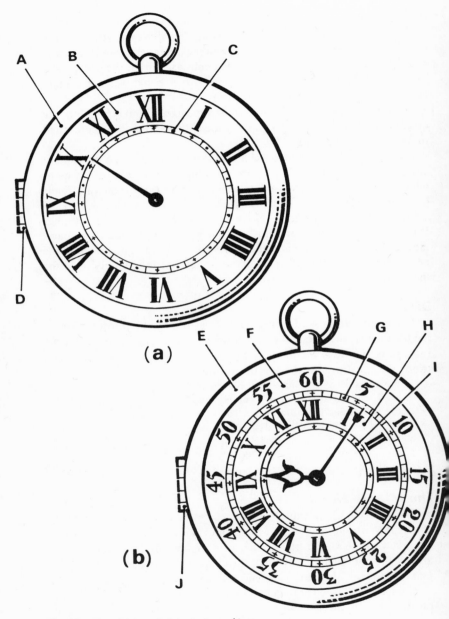

Fig. 23. The addition of dial minute markings.

82

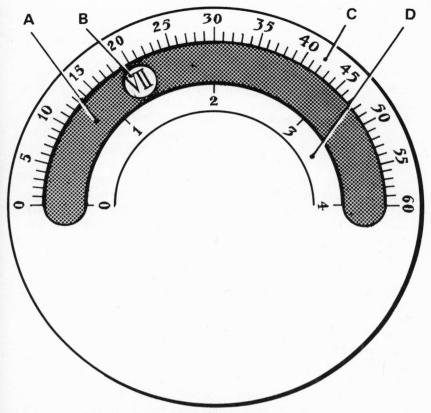

Fig. 24. Wandering hour dial. The time illustrated is 7:20.
- (A) Rotating disc
- (B) Hour numeral in window
- (C) Minute divisions
- (D) Quarter hour divisions

The Wandering Hour Dial

During the last quarter of the seventeenth century the wandering hour dial, Fig. 24, was in use in Holland, England and Germany. Its popularity was greatest in Holland and it continued to be fitted to Dutch watches well after 1700. It was also known as the floating hour dial, and, less frequently, watches with these dials were referred to as chronoscopes.

In the upper half of the dial was a semi-circular aperture. The outer edge was marked with sixty minute divisions, and Arabic numerals 0 to 60 were used at every fifth mark. The inner edge of the aperture was divided into four divisions, each representing a quarter of an hour, and again Arabic numerals were used, this time 0 to 4.

Beneath the dial a disc rotated and was viewed through the semi-circular aperture. In the disc was a window through which a Roman numeral, indicating the hour, could be seen. The disc rotated clockwise, taking the Roman hour numeral with it, and completed the half circle in one hour. Using a mark on the window edge as a pointer the owner could read the number of minutes past the hour at a glance at any time.

When the disc had completed its half revolution the window and Roman numeral disappeared from sight adjacent to the Arabic numeral 60, and a second window appeared, at the numeral 0, through which could be seen the Roman numeral of the succeeding hour, and the cycle repeated itself.

Behind the revolving disc, and to one side of each window, were two small revolving discs each with six teeth. One disc was marked with even numbers and the other with odd numbers. When any hour was complete and the numeral disappeared from view, a fixed pin turned the disc one tooth and positioned, the next odd or even hour numeral ready for display when required.

In the meantime, diametrically across the dial, a second window appeared behind which was the new hour following in correct numerical sequence.

A characteristic of English wandering hour watches was their reference to the royal family. Dials were invariably engraved with portraits of James II, Mary or Anne, or with their heraldic insignia. The reason for this remains a mystery.

The Sun and Moon Dial

A sun and moon dial watch had a champlevé dial with a semi-circular aperture in the upper half, Fig. 25. Behind the aperture, and concentric with the dial, was a disc that rotated clockwise once in twenty-four hours. Marked on the disc, diametrically opposite each other, were the sun and the moon, each with their own pointer. Around the curve of the aperture the dial was engraved with Roman numerals VI to XII, and I to VI, representing a cycle of twenty-four hours. Towards the outer edge of the dial was a minute ring with Arabic numerals 5 to 60, marked at intervals of five minutes, from which the divisions were read as indicated by a minute hand.

Fig. 25. Sun and moon dial. Time illustrated is 5:25 p.m.

At 6:00 a.m. the minute hand was at XII, and the sun's pointer was opposite VI on the left of the dial. Throughout the following twelve hours the disc rotated taking the sun with it until finally the sun's pointer coincided with VI on the right of the dial when the time was 6:00 p.m.

At that precise moment the pointer on the moon was exactly opposite VI on the left of the dial and the cycle was repeated to complete the full twenty-four hours.

The time illustrated in the drawing is 5:25 p.m.

The revolving disc added color to an already decorative watch. It was usual for the sun to be gilt against a background of silver, and the moon with its attendant stars to be silver on a deep blue sky.

The Six Hour Dial

The six hour dial watch, Fig. 26, was so called because it had only six hour markings in the chapter ring, i.e. Roman numerals I to VI, superimposed by Arabic numbers 7 to 12. Close to the edge of the dial was a minute ring which was marked with thirty divisions between

Fig. 26. Six hour dial. Time illustrated is 4:30 or 10:30.

each pair of chapters, each division representing two minutes. A single hand was used and the train was so arranged that the hand completed a full circle in six hours. It was therefore possible to read the time to within two minutes by the use of one hand only.

After the hand had travelled a full circle indicating time by the Roman numerals, its second revolution related to the Arabic figures. The wearer had to decide which set of numerals was appropriate at each reading. In the drawing the indicated time is thirty minutes past 4 o'clock or thirty minutes past 10 o'clock.

The Differential Dial

The differential dial watch, Fig. 27, is extremely rare and only a few are known to exist. It was a simple and ingenious arrangement.

Close to the outer edge was a minute ring with Arabic numerals 15, 30, 45 and 60 positioned at the quarters. The watch was fitted with a single hand that rotated once round the dial in an hour. In the center of the dial was a revolving disc engraved with Roman chapters I to XII. The disc rotated in a clockwise direction at a speed one twelfth less

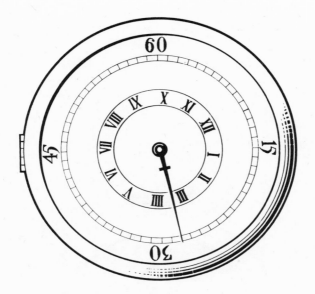

Fig. 27. Differential dial. Time illustrated is 3:28 a.m. or p.m.

than that of the hand. This meant that during the time the hour hand was completing one revolution, the disc was slowly falling back until, when the hand returned to its starting point, the chapter that was originally beneath the hand had been replaced by the succeeding chapter.

The wearer read the time by noting the Roman chapter that was trailing behind the hand, and then reading the number of minutes on the minute ring that are indicated by the hand. The time illustrated in the drawing is 3:28 a.m. or p.m.

The Champlevé Dial

A type of champlevé dial was in use during the early part of the seventeenth century but in limited numbers. During the second half of the century it became more common until, by 1675, it was in general use in England and remained so until the end of the century.

This dial was nearly always made of gold or silver. Metal was removed from the chapter ring with a graver leaving twelve polished cartouches or plaques standing in relief against a matt background. In

Fig. 28a. Silver pair-cased verge escapement watch with silver champlevé dial. The brass beetle and poker hands are unusual. Diameter 2¼ in. Signature William Holloway. London. Circa 1710.

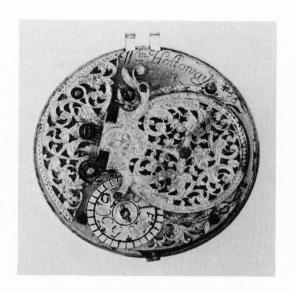

Fig. 28b. Top plate view of movement.

Fig. 28c. Side view of movement.

Fig. 29a. Gold repoussé pair-cased verge escapement watch showing the gold champlevé dial with blued steel beetle and poker hands. Diameter 1⅞ in. Signature John Ellicott. London. Hallmarked London 1735.

Fig. 29b. Back of watch case.

Fig. 29c. Top plate view of movement. Note the grotesque mask at the foot of the balance cock.

Fig. 30a. Silver repoussé pair-cased verge escapement watch. The white enamel dial has an arcaded minute ring suggesting Dutch origin. Gilt hands. Diameter 2⅛ inches. Signature Rensman. London. Rensman is recorded by Baillie as working in Zwol, Holland. Circa 1720.

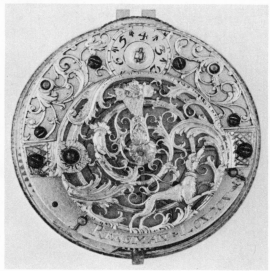

Fig. 30b. Back of watch case.

Fig. 30c. Top plate view of movement. Cast silver balance bridge.

Fig. 31.

Top left.
French striking watch with single hour hand. Movement with fusee and chain. Balance 3.0 cm diameter. Silver case and dial. Diameter 5.6 cm. Late 17th century.

Top right.
Silver cased watch with typical Dutch arcaded dial with date aperture. Diameter 5.7 cm. Signature Jacobus Vand. Heoge (Hague). Circa 1785.

Middle left.
Silver cased alarm watch with single hour hand. London made. Diameter 5.7 cm. Circa 1700.

Middle right.
Silver cased watch with sun and moon dial and date aperture. Diameter 5.5 cm. Signature Halsted. London. Circa 1685.

Bottom left.
Silver cased alarm watch with single hour hand and enamel dial. Diameter 5.6 cm. Circa 1700.

Bottom right.
Verge escapement watch with fusee and chain. Gilt and enamel dial with single hour hand. Note Roman IV instead of the more usual IIII. Diameter 6.0 cm. Signature Balthazar Martinot. Paris. Martinot was watchmaker to Louis XIII. Circa 1625.

these plaques the chapters were engraved and then filled with hot colored wax, usually black.

The center of the dial, inside the hour ring, was removed and a metal disc, slightly larger in diameter than the hole, was secured beneath the dial plate. On this center disc the watchmaker engraved his signature and town. A few subsidiary seconds dials appeared about 1680.

The White Enamel Dial

Shortly after 1675 white enamel dials began to appear in Europe and in England, but the quality of the enamelling was poor. The surface contained small indentations and the finish was cloudy. They lacked the luster that was to become characteristic of white enamel dials of the middle eighteenth century.

In France and Switzerland before 1700 white enamel dials seem to have been almost confined to watches with enamel cases. It was not until the early years of the eighteenth century that they became more widely used.

The first to appear in France were the thirteen piece dials. Each hour numeral had its own large and separate enamel plaque that was stuck onto the enamelled dial plate. The numerals or chapters were invariably blue whereas in Switzerland any color other than black was rare. Near the end of the seventeenth century the plaques became smaller and other dials presented their chapters on an enamel ring mounted on a gilt dial plate.

After 1700 the practice of adhering the chapter plaques to the plate was discontinued but the illusion was maintained by making the domed plaques part of the dial and outlining them with a fine line of black paint. The enamel plaque dials are rare after 1725.

In England the use of white enamel dials was even more limited and it was not until about 1725 that their numbers increased appreciably. About that time Graham decided to use them as a standard fitting to the majority of his watches. The markings were similar to those of the champlevé dial but without the half and quarter hour divisions.

Dutch Dials

A distinctive feature of Dutch dials, no matter whether they were champlevé or enamel, was the arcaded or wavy minute ring that had twelve small arches each positioned between a pair of hour markings.

Fig. 32. Hands.
    (a)   English (tulip), circa 1680
    (b)   Dutch, circa 1685
    (c)   English, circa 1685
    (d)   English (beetle and poker), circa 1690
    (e)   French, circa 1720

In other respects the Dutch seemed content to follow the French and English styles.

Hands

When English watchmakers introduced the minute hand the most popular design was the tulip, Fig. 32, (a), of which there were numerous variations. About 1690 a new design was introduced which remained in regular use until the end of the eighteenth century. This was the "beetle and poker," (d), so called because of its resemblance to a stag beetle and a fireside poker. The very early hands were finished black but by the end of the seventeenth century blued steel was being widely applied. With white enamel dials it was usual to fit hands of gold.

The Dutch were not long after the British in introducing minute hands. A typical example of their early pierced designs is shown in (b).

French watchmakers favored winding their movements from the front instead of through the back of the case. Provision was made for the winding square to protrude through the boss that carried the single hour hand. The French reluctance to give up this convenient method of winding is reflected by the continual use of the single hand up to about 1725. Watches with minute hands are rare before 1710. After this time, the hands were made of steel or brass-gilt and fashioned into a broad pierced design that lacked refinement, (e).

When the addition of the minute hand effectively prevented winding from taking place at the center, French watchmakers made provision for a keyhole elsewhere on the dial wherever it happened to be needed with complete disregard to decoration, numerals or appearance.

The first watches with minute hands had no motion work and the wearer had to set the two hands independently by pushing them round by finger as had been the practice with single hand watches.

Pendants

Until about 1675 pendants consisted of a loose fitting ring passing through a hole drilled from side to side through a small spherical knob at the top of the case. It was about this time that Charles II made popular the long waistcoat among the English gentry and it became fashionable to wear watches in a waistcoat pocket. The loose pendant ring was then replaced by the pivoted loop, or bow, as it became known. The early ones were oval and then later developed into what closely resembled a stirrup.

Fakes

The finest watches were undoubtedly those made in London and any watch with a dial so marked, and bearing the maker's name, was greatly prized. It is not surprising therefore that unscrupulous attempts were made to produce watches that appeared to have originated in London.

There were many such fakes after 1700, most of them from Holland. Usually the dials were typically Dutch with an arcaded minute ring, but bearing the name of a leading London maker, Tompion and Quare being the most popular, doubtless because they fetched the highest price. The balance is almost invariably supported by a bridge instead of a cock.

Many of these watches are of poor quality but even so after two hundred years they possess a very real collector's value.

CHAPTER 5
The Marine Chronometer
(1725-1785)

DURING the fifteenth century mariners began sailing their ships into uncharted waters. Wind was their only means of propulsion and all too often was the cause of their destruction. They spent weeks at sea without sight of land. With the help of astronomers these explorers taught themselves to navigate by observing the position of the sun and the stars. At its best this method of navigation was only approximate, and when settlers began sailing to new lands and trade routes were opened there was a real and urgent need for more accurate navigation.

The surface of the earth is considered to have two sets of lines running round it. Those lines that pass through the north and south poles are known as longitude, and those that circle the earth at right angles to the lines of longitude are known as latitude. For the purpose of plotting location it is convenient to take a map of the world and lay it flat.

The line of longitude that runs through Greenwich, London, is the meridian 0°, and the remaining lines of longitude are referred to by their distance, in degrees, east or west of 0° up to 180°.

The line of latitude that runs midway between the two poles is 0° and is called the equator. The other lines of latitude are referred to by their distance, in degrees, north or south of the equator up to 90°.

It can be seen that if both longitude and latitude are known, an exact position can be plotted on a map. By means of a sextant navigators are able to make astronomical observations on the sun and the stars and produce mathematical computations that tell them their latitude and local time, but observations are of little help in determining the longitude.

The earth rotates about an axis that passes through the two poles, and in twenty-four hours completes a full turn of 360°.

If	24 hours	= 360°
then	1 hour	= 15°
	4 minutes	= 1°
	1 minute	= ¼° or 15'

and 15' is nearly equivalent to fifteen nautical miles at the equator.

The time at Greenwich has been internationally accepted as the standard and is known as Greenwich Mean Time (G.M.T.). All places on longitude 0° have the same G.M.T.

It follows that the difference between local time and G.M.T. can be converted into distance which will be a number of degrees longitude east or west of 0°. Local time can be accurately calculated when astronomical readings for finding latitude are taken; all that is needed is some means of knowing G.M.T. The only way was by carrying an accurate timepiece on board ship. There were clocks capable of maintaining time within the limits required but they were controlled by long pendulums, an impossible arrangement at sea.

During the latter part of the sixteenth century Spain was fast becoming an important maritime nation and Philip II recognized the tremendous advantage his sea-going captains would have over those of other nations if they had a means of calculating accurately their longitudinal position. In 1598 he offered a large sum of money to anyone who could supply the means to this end but no one could.

More than half a century passed and then, shortly after he came to the English throne in 1660, Charles II ordered the construction of Greenwich Observatory to "rectify the tables of the motions of the heavens, and the places of the fixed stars, so as to find out the so-much desired longitude of places for perfecting the art of navigation."

Another half century passed and mariners were no nearer to having their problem solved. Then, a body of scientists, including Sir Isaac Newton, submitted their recommendations to Parliament and in 1714 an act was passed by the British Government "for providing a publick reward for such person or persons as shall discover the longitude."

A Royal Commission was set up. It was decided that the reward would be paid to anyone producing a timepiece that kept within close limits during the six weeks sea voyage from England to the West Indies. The scale approved by Parliament was as follows:

1. £ 10,000: within one degree of longitude
2. £ 15,000: within two-thirds degree of longitude
3. £ 20,000: within half degree of longitude

We have seen that to calculate longitude to within half a degree it is necessary that the timekeeper be accurate to within two minutes. To achieve this, throughout a journey of six weeks, means that any variation must not exceed three seconds each day.

$$2 \text{ minutes } = 120 \text{ seconds}$$
$$\div 6 \text{ weeks } = 20 \text{ seconds a week}$$
or approximately 3 seconds a day

A Board of Longitude was formed whose function was to scrutinize any applications and to investigate subsequent claims.

England's action was followed by other seafaring nations. The Dutch authorities offered a large financial reward for a means of measuring longitude and in 1720 the Paris Academy of Science offered a money prize for the same purpose. Whichever nation was first in possessing such an instrument would undoubtedly lead the world in navigation at sea.

These generous money prizes were a great incentive to clock and watch makers, and the names of many eminent craftsmen will always be associated with the development of the marine timekeeper, or chronometer, as it came to be called. In seeking a way to produce an accurate timekeeper for use at sea watchmakers applied the best of their many inventions to precision pocket watches which explains their rapid development during the second half of the eighteenth century.

The first man to provide a solution to the problem was an Englishman, John Harrison. The achievement took over thirty years to accomplish during which he designed and built five marine timekeepers. They are known today as Harrison's No. 1, No. 2, No. 3, No. 4 and No. 5. It was the fourth instrument that finally won for him the reward.

Harrison had been brought up to carry on his father's carpentry business but at an early age he demonstrated his aptitude for mechanics by cleaning and repairing clocks and watches. He was completely self-taught. Shortly after reaching the age of twenty-one he began making clocks, and by the time he reached the age of twenty-five he was designing horological improvements. Then he became interested in the longitude problem. The magnitude of the prize money offered by the government showed how desperate was the need, and the idea of being the first to produce a solution presented itself as a personal challenge. During the next few years most of Harrison's time was spent working on the design of a marine timepiece until, in 1728, he travelled to London with drawings and some of his inventions, including the famous gridiron temperature compensated pendulum, as evidence of his ability.

The Board of Longitude appointed George Graham to carry out a preliminary interview. Graham was very impressed with Harrison's ideas and his standard of workmanship and advised him to return home and produce a timekeeper that could be submitted to the board for test. He loaned Harrison £200 unconditionally and without interest or surety to help him with his research.

Greatly encouraged by Graham's help and advice, Harrison returned to his home in Yorkshire and divided his time between repair work and designing and constructing a marine timekeeper.

Harrison's No. 1 (1728-1735)

The first instrument took seven years to build. It was a bulky arrangement mounted in a wooden frame about two feet in length and weighing over seventy pounds. The movement employed the now famous ''grasshopper'' escapement and had two large balances vertically mounted which oscillated in opposing directions to cancel out interferences caused by the motion of a ship. Two mainsprings provided the power through a centrally placed fusee, and the winding mechanism incorporated Harrison's maintaining power.

Winding a fusee involved placing a key on the squared end of the fusee arbor and turning the fusee in the direction opposite to normal rotation. This immediately removed power from the great wheel and the movement stopped. Harrison devised a method of maintaining power to the great wheel during winding by modifying the design of the fusee.

Between the great wheel and the fusee cone he fitted a ratchet wheel that was loose on the fusee arbor. The drive from the fusee was transmitted to the ratchet wheel through a pawl (pall) and ratchet, and from the ratchet wheel to the great wheel by means of a coupling spring that was kept under tension. A click engaged with the teeth of the ratchet wheel to prevent reverse rotation.

When winding took place and the fusee no longer acted as a driving force there was sufficient tension in the coupling spring to supply the great wheel with power throughout the duration of the winding. The device became known as Harrison's maintaining power.

With the exception of the escape wheel, the train in Harrison's No. 1 was made of wood, the oak teeth being made in sets of four and inserted into the rim. The rollers of the lantern pinions were made of lignum vitae because of its extreme hardness and resistance to wear. Friction wheels were used to support the pivots. This was an arrangement, invented by Henry Sully, where the rims of three or four wheels, or segments, were brought together close enough to provide a location for the pivot with minimum bearing surface. The movement required no lubrication.

Harrison was the first to provide compensation for changes in rate brought about by variation of temperature. The problem was that metals expand when heated and contract when cooled. Different metals have different co-efficients of expansion, i.e. they expand or contract in different amounts for a given rise or fall in temperature. Brass, for example, expands and contracts more than steel.

If the pendulum of a clock is subjected to a rise in temperature it will expand and increase in length, and the clock will slow down. The gridiron is an arrangement of vertically mounted steel and brass rods placed alternately side by side. Five steel rods and four brass rods are used and the total length of each metal is in the proportion of 5:3 which is approximately the ratio of their co-efficients of expansion. During changes in temperature the two rates of expansion or contraction cancel each other and the length of the pendulum remains constant.

A sprung balance is affected in a similar manner and a rise in temperature will slow the movement down. Harrison compensated for expansion and contraction by employing his gridiron principle to vary the effective length of the balance spring.

In 1736, the year after Harrison completed his first instrument, he was granted permission to take it on board a ship of the King's fleet and to sail with it from England to Lisbon. The trial lasted the duration of the voyage and when it was over the instrument indicated a degree of error equivalent to less than five miles. The Board of Longitude was so impressed by this outstanding performance that it advanced Harrison £500 to enable him to continue with his research.

Harrison's No. 2 (1736-1739)

The second instrument was similar in design to the first but Harrison abandoned the use of wood in favor of metal, resulting in a movement, without its case, weighing over one hundred pounds. It incorporated a remontoire. This was an arrangement whereby the escape wheel was driven by two helical springs that were wound by the mainspring sixteen times an hour. The effect was to provide the escape wheel with a driving force that remained constant.

In 1739, when the instrument was finished, England and Spain were at war, and the British government fearing that the timekeeper might be captured would not allow a trial to be carried out on the high seas. Instead, tests were made in London, the results indicating that it was capable of even greater accuracy than Harrison's No. 1.

Harrison's No. 3 (1740-1757)

The third timekeeper was less complicated and not as large as its predecessors. As before, two balance wheels were used but this time they were controlled by a single spiral spring. Harrison adopted a new method of compensating for changes in temperature and it may well have been this feature that caused him to spend seventeen years in the construction of the timekeeper. The compensator was a bimetallic strip consisting of two flat pieces of brass and steel riveted together. One end of the strip was rigidly held to the plate, and the other end was free. Because of the different co-efficients of expansion of the two metals, changes in temperature caused the strip to bend. When the temperature rose, the free end moved in one direction, and when the temperature fell, the strip bent in the opposite direction. The free end carried two small curb pins set close together. Between the two pins passed the outer end of the balance spring. When the temperature changed, the end of the strip carried the two pins along the balance spring which altered its effective length. The rate was thus increased or decreased accordingly. This arrangement became known as the compensation curb and continued to be used in precision watches for the next one hundred years.

Harrison had ideas for a fourth timekeeper that were completely different from the three that he had already made. He notified the Board of Longitude of the completion of the third timekeeper but asked that he be allowed to put his new ideas into practice before making any further trials.

In recognition of his work and for producing the most useful invention of the year, the Royal Society, in 1749, awarded Harrison their annual gold medal.

Harrison's No. 4 (1757-1759)

While Harrison was making his third marine timekeeper he began thinking about designing a very much smaller instrument and dispensing with the heavy cumbersome framework and its proportionately large components. In 1753 he arranged with John Jeffreys to make a pocket watch incorporating these new ideas but it was found impossible to make a remontoire small enough. This prototype watch was completed but Harrison realized it was too large to be successful. As soon as the third timekeeper was finished he started work on his fourth and completed it in two years.

Throughout his horological career Harrison went to great lengths to ensure that all moving parts in his timekeepers were designed to function with the minimum of surface friction. This principle was well demonstrated in his fourth instrument.

The movement was fitted with a fusee to which was coupled Harrison's own maintaining power mechanism. Train wheel pivots were located in ruby jewels that had end stones of diamond. Coupled to the fourth wheel was a very fine remontoire that operated every seven and a half seconds. The escapement resembled a verge but was considerably modified and refined with very small diamond pallets. The drop of each escape wheel tooth was only one six-thousandth part of an inch which made for silent running. The single steel balance measured a little under two and one quarter inches in diameter and beat five times a second. The watch was compensated for changes in temperature by means of a compensation curb acting on the balance spring. The dial carried a center seconds hand.

This beautiful piece of precision work in a silver pair-case, a little less than five and one quarter inches in diameter, eventually won for him the £20,000 reward offered by the British government.

Harrison notified the Board of Longitude of the completion of his fourth timekeeper and asked that it be put on trial under the terms of the act. There was considerable delay before arrangements were finalized and two years elapsed before trials began. Harrison was by then sixty-seven years of age and he felt he was too old to undertake the sea voyage with its attendant responsibilities, so he sent his son William.

The British government had arranged for the trials to take place on board the "Deptford," and on November 18th 1761 William embarked at Portsmouth bound for Jamaica. The ship was due to call at Madeira for supplies, and after eighteen days by conventional navigation the position of the ship was logged as 13° 15' west of Portsmouth. Harrison's instrument indicated the ship was 15° 19', and William advised the captain to change course. At first the captain refused but William pointed out that his refusal would destroy the purpose of the trial and that the performance of the timekeeper throughout the voyage would never be known. The captain finally gave in and changed course. Late the following day the island was sighted almost straight ahead. It was subsequently reckoned that had the ship remained on its original course it would have passed too far away from the island for the crew to sight it.

The amount of error allowed by the act was three seconds a day. The voyage to Jamaica lasted sixty-one days, and at the end Harrison's instrument was only five seconds slow which, when converted into distance, represents approximately one and a half miles in the latitude of Jamaica. A most remarkable and outstanding performance. After a lifetime of devoted research Harrison had shown the world that it was possible to calculate longitude at sea with great accuracy.

On January 28th 1762 William sailed for Portsmouth on board the "Merlin." The ship encountered some extremely rough weather and was frequently blown off course. By the time he arrived back in England five months had elapsed since his departure in the "Deptford." In all that time the error of the instrument was only one minute and fifty-three and a half seconds, the equivalent of 18' of longitude in the latitude of Portsmouth.

In those days an accuracy of one minute a day had become commonplace with high grade watches but the performance of Harrison's instrument was undreamed of. One can understand the reluctance of the British government to pay the £20,000 reward for a single trial that had produced what was thought to be an unobtainable result. An advance of £5,000 was paid on the understanding that a second trial be undertaken.

It was not until 1764 that arrangements were finalized for another trial. The Board of Longitude appointed Dr. Maskelyne, the astronomer royal, to act as its representative and to accompany William on the voyage as witness to the performance of the instrument. On March 28th 1764 the two men embarked on the man-of-war "Tartar" bound for Barbados, a journey that lasted forty-six days. On June 4th, three weeks after their arrival at Barbados, they sailed for England on the "New Elizabeth," the return voyage taking forty-four days.

During their one hundred and twelve days of absence the timekeeper had gained one hundred and sixty-six seconds, a little more than one second a day.

The reliability and accuracy of Harrison's timekeeper was proven and members of the board were unhesitatingly unanimous in declaring him fully entitled to the government reward. Even so, they were still not satisfied. Instead of paying Harrison the balance of the £20,000, another advance of £5,000 was made on the understanding that he give full and precise details of how the instrument was made.

A sub-committee was formed, headed by Dr. Maskelyne and consisting of William Ludlam, professor of mathematics at Cambridge University, and five prominent London makers, Thomas Mudge, Larcum Kendall, John Bird, William Mathews and John Mitchell.

With Harrison's help the committee studied the mechanics of the instrument until they were satisfied that they understood the manufacturing processes involved. Further delay was then caused when the Board of Longitude asked Kendall to make a duplicate instrument, presumably to assess its adaptability to production methods. Kendall completed the task in 1769 for which he was paid £450. Even at this stage there was reluctance on the part of the government to pay the reward money to Harrison.

Harrison's No. 5 (1768-1772)

In the meantime Harrison made yet another timekeeper. He was in his seventy-ninth year when it was completed, and to bring an end to the bickering that had developed between the Board of Longitude and himself he appealed to King George III to take his latest piece of work and subject it to trial in his private observatory at Kew. The king agreed and over a period of ten weeks the instrument maintained accuracy to within four and a half seconds. In the face of this overwhelming evidence the king failed to see why the British government should not honor its agreement, and, under the weight of his influence, Harrison received, in 1773, the balance of the £20,000 reward. He died three years later at the age of eighty-three having spent most of his working life in solving the problem of calculating longitude at sea.

Harrison's marine timekeepers are still going. The first four can be seen in the National Maritime Museum, Greenwich, London, and the fifth instrument is on display in the Guildhall Museum, London, and is the property of the Worshipful Company of Clockmakers.

The duplicate of Harrison's No. 4, made by Kendall for the board, sailed with Captain Cook on his famous three year voyage around the South Pole, and performed with a degree of accuracy equal to that of the original. It is fitting that the final resting place of this instrument is next to No. 4 at Greenwich.

Kendall subsequently made two more instruments according to his own more simplified design but their performance was of a lower standard. Captain Bligh had one of them aboard the ''Bounty'' when his crew mutinied and captured the ship. After a long and dramatic career at sea the instrument finally returned to England in 1843 and can now be seen in the Royal United Services Institution at Whitehall, London.

After Harrison's death his son William made a sixth instrument but regrettably its whereabouts is unknown.

In pursuing the story of the development of the marine chronometer we must consider the invaluable work of three distinguished men who lived on after Harrison died. One of them, Pierre Le Roy, lived in France and was unaware of Harrison's inventions. The remaining two were John Arnold and Thomas Earnshaw, both of whom made valuable contributions toward facilitating the commercial production of Harrison's achievement.

Pierre Le Roy (1717-1785)

Pierre Le Roy and his father Julien are, without question, the most famous of all French horologists. When Pierre was about twenty-five years of age he began taking an interest in the problems associated with accurate calculations of longitude at sea. In 1748 he designed an entirely new form of escapement which he called a detent escapement. Its particular attribute was its ability to swing almost without mechanical interference and for this reason it became known as a detached form of escapement.

It was this arrangement, but in a much more sophisticated form, that ultimately became the regular type of escapement used internationally in marine chronometers.

Le Roy continued with his experiments and by 1766 he produced a marine watch that was so elegant and accurate that it was demonstrated to Louis XV.

The watch contained a much improved detent escapement and a completely new method of temperature compensation. Instead of using Harrison's method of automatically adjusting the effective length of the balance spring, Le Roy designed an arrangement whereby the effective diameter of the balance itself was altered. This method of compensation proved to be superior.

A small thermometer, containing alcohol and mercury, was applied to the balance in such a way that a rise in temperature caused the mercury to move towards the center and thereby maintain the rate, whereas a decrease caused the reverse action to occur. This was the first attempt to embody the means of compensation within the balance, and proof of its superiority is evident in modern precision watches. It is always the balance that provides compensation.

Two spiral isochronous springs were fitted to the balance, and timing screws were fitted to the rim to adjust the rate. Le Roy avoided the possibility of the balance pivots meeting with resistance from thickening oil by arranging for them to function between rollers.

So sure was Le Roy that the merits of his escapement and balance would alone produce the accuracy required for the calculation of longitude that he dispensed with refinements in the train. There was no fusee, no remontoire and no jewelled pivot holes.

The French government arranged for a trial at sea on board the "Aurore." The trial was far less demanding than that to which Harrison's No. 4 had been subjected, but nevertheless Le Roy's "montre marine" completely vindicated itself. It was at least equal in performance to Harrison's No. 4.

Le Roy's watch is now in the custody of the Conservatoire des Arts et Métiers in Paris.

John Arnold (1736-1799)

John Arnold first began taking an interest in the calculation of longitude at sea in 1764. By 1770 he completed his first chronometer and fitted it with a pivoted detent escapement of his own design. The instrument was used on the "Resolution" when Captain Cook made his second voyage in 1772 but it failed to conform to the standard required by the Board of Longitude.

The pivoted detent never gained popularity in England; it was more favored in Europe where it was known as the bascule.

During the next four years Arnold experimented with different forms of pivoted detent and made several pocket chronometers. In 1776 he was the first to fit balances with helical springs and six years later, after a succession of experiments, he found that by shaping the springs with end curves he achieved isochronism, Fig. 33. Many of these springs were made of gold. Helical springs in chronometers became standard practice and have remained in use through the years.

In 1773 Arnold had begun experimenting with bimetallic compensators. During the years 1775 to 1778 he produced twelve pocket

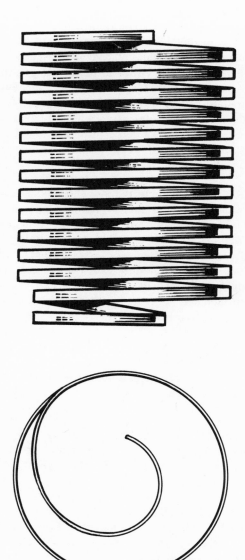

Fig. 33. Arnold's helical spring with end curves.

chronometers each fitted with a spiral bimetallic coil secured to the balance. Attached to the coil was an arrangement of levers which, when moved, caused two weights, placed diametrically opposite each other, to move away from or closer to the center of the balance.

One of these chronometers, No. 36 which was made in 1776, was tested at Greenwich, London, by being worn for thirteen months. At the end of this period the total error was only two minutes and thirty-three seconds, a remarkable performance.

During the following two years Arnold made twenty more chronometers in which he substituted two short bars for the bimetallic coil.

From 1779 to 1782 he made forty more chronometers and replaced the bars with bimetallic strips shaped like an elongated letter S.

Arnold's final method of compensation was to dispense entirely with moving weights. Instead he devised a bimetallic balance, the first of its kind. He took four strips, two of brass and two of steel, and shaped each to almost a semi-circle. Each brass strip was then soldered to the outside of a steel strip and the two assemblies were screwed, one to each end of the balance transverse bar. This was the forerunner of the modern bimetallic balance.

In the meantime Arnold had continued with his experiments with detent escapements and by 1780 he had produced his final arrangement which was a spring detent.

Arnold's method of production was to employ men, each a specialist in the manufacture of a particular component, while he engaged himself with final assembly and adjustment.

Thomas Earnshaw (1749-1829)

In 1780 Thomas Earnshaw designed a spring detent escapement. He showed his invention to his employer who advised him to apply for a patent, but Earnshaw had insufficient money to cover the cost. Thomas Wright, a customer, offered to pay for the patent providing he was first allowed to test a chronometer that was fitted with Earnshaw's device. This was agreed upon, but Wright kept the chonometer for three years before making application for the patent during which time Arnold made known details of his own spring detent.

Earnshaw immediately accused Arnold of stealing the idea saying that he must have acquired the knowledge from Brockbank or Wright.

It is possible that the two men produced near identical designs

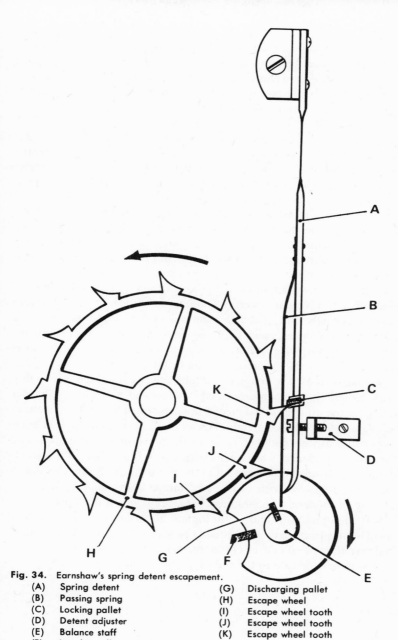

Fig. 34. Earnshaw's spring detent escapement.

(A)	Spring detent	(G)	Discharging pallet
(B)	Passing spring	(H)	Escape wheel
(C)	Locking pallet	(I)	Escape wheel tooth
(D)	Detent adjuster	(J)	Escape wheel tooth
(E)	Balance staff	(K)	Escape wheel tooth
(F)	Impulse pallet		

almost simultaneously, but it is now most unlikely that the facts about the case will ever be known. Of the two designs Earnshaw's became the standard fitting in chronometers. Its function is shown in Fig. 34.

Movement of the escape wheel H is arrested by locking pallet C engaging with tooth K. When the balance rotates clockwise the discharging pallet G pushes to one side the passing spring B, usually made of gold and hence frequently referred to as the gold spring. This action in turn deflects the spring detent A. Locking pallet C is thereby moved clear of tooth K and the escape wheel turns in a counter clockwise direction. Tooth I gives an impulse to the impulse pallet F and then tooth J is arrested by locking pallet C.

At the end of its swing the balance reverses direction and when the discharging pallet G meets the passing spring B, the spring, being very light, offers no resistance to G which continues with its swing without interference to C. When the swing is complete and the balance once again turns clockwise, the cycle is repeated.

Arnold's spring detent differs principally in that the relative positions of A and B are in reverse. The release of the escape wheel teeth takes place when the balance rotates counter clockwise and C is moved toward the escape wheel instead of away from it. The escape wheel turns clockwise. It is arrested by locking pallet C which makes contact with a small shoulder on the tip of each tooth.

Earnshaw took advantage of Arnold's ten years of experimenting with bimetallic compensators and commenced his research by developing the bimetallic balance. Earnshaw introduced the system of fusing together the two metals. His method was to pour molten brass over a disc of steel and then machine the result in a lathe until he had produced a balance wheel whose rim was bimetallic. Two slots, diametrically opposite, were cut in the rim to allow the two halves of the circle to move with changes of temperature. In principle, the making of modern compensation balances is much the same.

It is the opinion of many horological historians that John Arnold and Thomas Earnshaw share equally in making possible the commercial manufacture of marine chronometers and the production of precision watches for sale to the public at moderate prices.

Fig. 35a. Very large marine chronometer signed on the dial Brockbanks, London. Despite its size, it has a duration of one day. Brockbanks were among the earliest of English makers. This chronometer was made around 1800 and has an enamel dial of great clarity.

Fig. 35b. The frosted plates add strikingly to the appearance of the movement. Note the three-armed balance which is characteristic of much of this maker's work. The escapement is Thomas Earnshaw's spring detent. Diameter of bezel 143 mm. Box measures 228 mm. square.

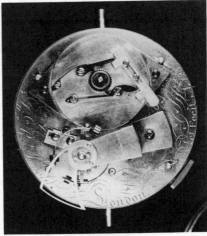

Fig. 36a. A two-day marine chronometer signed on the dial Jon R. Arnold, London. Invt et Fecit. 425. This is a technically interesting machine dating from 1813 or perhaps earlier. It is decidedly experimental by nature and displays a measure of inventive genius inherited by the son of a famous father. The reason for the eccentric chapter is that the movement beneath has a large spring barrel, thus doing away with a fusee.

Fig. 36b. The top plate view of movement. The large spring barrel has two clicks mounted upon it. Within is a very long steel spring. The cock carries a guard upon it to protect the balance when the movement is being removed from the bowl. The balance is a form of the so-called Z-type with four screwed weights. The adjustable clamp on the top plate will hold one end of the helical spring.

Fig. 36c. Side view of movement. The slot for John Arnold's form of spring detent is clearly seen. Between the plates is an escape wheel with cycloidal teeth which gives impulse to the balance. This chronometer became the property of the admiralty and served aboard the "Magicienne" on the Indian station between 1816 and 1819. Its last service at sea was in 1857 aboard H.M.S. "Waterloo," according to admiralty records, and it was finally cut off the books in 1862 when it was given with 30 in exchange for a new chronometer.

Fig. 37a. A very fine small eight-day marine chronometer signed upon the dial Barrauds, London. This machine dates from about 1818. It was recovered a few years ago from India and may have been the property of the Hon. East India Company. The dial displays several beautiful features characteristic of early chronometers such as the narrow bezel and domed glass. The gimbal fits closely to the bezel and very snugly within the mahogany box. The aperture in the dial reveals the state of wind. The words "up, 1, 2, 3," etc., appear by turns until finally "wind up" and "down" appear.

Fig. 37b. The movement showing its raised barrel bridge and full plate construction. Note the Pennington balance and Pennington's method of fitting the detent of the Earnshaw escapement into a slot. The winding square carries a Barrauds patent winder fixed permanently in position.

Fig. 37c. The movement showing the Pennington balance in close-up. In design, it anticipated Eiffe's and Molyneux's auxiliary balances which appeared about 1840. Diameter of bezel 99 mm. Box measures 135 x 135 x 140 mm.

Fig. 38a. A two-day marine chronometer in a mahogany box with sliding lid. Dial carries up-and-down quadrant and blued steel hands. Signature on the dial is Breguet Neveu & Cie. Dépot de la Marine.

120

Fig. 38b. Fusee movement with detachable platform. Earnshaw escapement with compensation balance and helical spring. The movement is mounted in a brass-gilt bowl with oval gimbal ring.

121

Fig. 39. A two-day marine chronometer signed on the dial Parkinson & Frodsham. The number 253 appears inside. This chronometer was sent by its makers at their own risk with W. E. Parry, the Arctic explorer, in 1819-1820. Subjected to extremely low temperatures it continued to perform steadily and was purchased by the admiralty upon its return. It also served on Parry's second voyage to the Arctic from 1821 to 1823. Thereafter it served in various ships and saw limited service at the Royal Observatory, Cape of Good Hope. In 1860 it went down aboard the gunboat "Jasner" but was later salvaged. The chronometer lay for many years regarded as "ruined and utterly useless" until it was disposed of in 1887. The record ends here, but its civilian owner (possibly the firm of Frodsham) restored it to working order and refinished the dial with two-color gold because it had been injured by sea water. Diameter of bezel 100 mm.

Fig. 40. Pocket chronometer by Thos. Giffin, London. 337. Britten (see Appendix 4, Bibliography, under Baillie) notes that this maker was in business about 1820 but little else is known of him. He probably made pocket chronometers for more famous watchmakers and this example bears some resemblance to those sold under Barrauds' name. The balance, with screwed weights around its rim, is more satisfactory for this kind of timekeeper because it must keep time in any position. Position error is far more difficult to remedy in a pocket chronometer fitted with a balance carrying segmental weights. Diameter of case 52 mm.

Fig. 41. A two-day marine chronometer signed on the dial Molyneux & Sons, 30 Southampton Row, London. 1558. The condition of this machine is entirely original. It dates from about the year 1831. The narrow bezel and domed glass are typical features of the period. The hour and minute hands are gold, the seconds and up and down indicator blued steel. Molyneux was regarded as an expert on Earnshaw's form of spring detent escapement as early as 1805 when he was nominated an adjudicator by the Board of Longitude. This chronometer has an Earnshaw escapement and a balance with segmental weights. The plates are lightly frosted. When this machine was put on a year-long trial in 1972-1973 it gained only 3 minutes 28 seconds, thus showing that these old chronometers can still give a fine performance. The bezel diameter is 115 mm. Box measurements are 153 x 153 x 163 mm.

Fig. 42. A small two-day marine chronometer of French manufacture by Winnerl, No. 441, in entirely original condition. Winnerl was apprenticed to Breguet before establishing himself independently in business in Paris in 1829. Even in wear, this chronometer gives a remarkably steady rate. European chronometer makers often favored a box with a circular glazed aperture protected by a slide, as in this example. Earnshaw escapement. Bezel diameter 78 mm. Box measures 147 x 147 x 140 mm.

Fig. 43. A two-day chronometer with Earnshaw escapement and free sprung compensation balance with wedge-shaped weights. Silvered dial, gold hands and up-and-down indicator. Signed Brockbanks and Atkins, London, No. 1000.

The label pasted in the lid of the mahogany box reads:

    Brockbanks & Atkins
    No. 6 Cowper's Court, Cornhill
    London
    1834

  General Directions for the Use of Chronometers.

Chronometers should be always kept in an horizontal position.

They should be wound up every Day, and as near the same hour as possible.

To wind Chronometers, turn them gently up on their Axis, holding them steadily with one Hand whilst winding with the other, then return them slowly into their former position.

Avoid giving the Chronometer any quick or sudden motion, and particularly a circular one, as this latter may cause an Error of several seconds, or perhaps stop it altogether.

Never open a Chronometer unless from absolute Necessity, and then carefully avoid touching the Seconds Hands.

Should a Chronometer stop by being let down or otherwise, hold it horizontally, and give it a short, brisk, circular motion, which will restore it again to action.

CHAPTER 6

The Development of Precision Watches
(1750-1830)

THE most important single contribution in the history of watch development was the invention of the balance spring in 1675; now one could measure time in minutes instead of having to approximate it between the hours. Then, in the eighteenth century, John Harrison demonstrated how time could be measured in seconds.

Without question the greatest number of advances ever made in the development of pocket watches took place during the eighty years from 1750 to 1830. Harrison's outstanding success with his No. 4 marine chronometer provided a tremendous stimulus for the inventive minds of leading horologists on both sides of the English Channel.

During this period men like Breguet, Arnold and Emery led others to produce watches capable of an accuracy far greater than was ever thought possible. Such a period of tremendous ingenuity and excitement cannot fail to capture one's interest and offer any discriminating collector a wealth of choice.

Movements

Watches from this period were made with full plate movements. All the wheels were contained between the plates, and the balance and cock were positioned outside. The English makers were stubborn in their insistence to continue fitting fusees and the general result was a thick watch.

In the meantime French makers had begun producing slim watches, and the new style quickly gained in popularity. By the turn of the century the horological lead held by England for so long was lost to her French rivals.

Color Plate I.

Upper left.
Gold and enamel watch in the form of a lyre. Case edged with pearls. The balance is visible beneath the strings.

Top center.
Gold and enamel beetle-shaped watch. The two wings are decorated with diamonds and are self-opening. Circa 1800.

Upper right.
Gold and enamel watch in the shape of a mandolin. The case is decorated with a pastoral scene. Swiss. Circa 1800.

Lower left.
Gold ring watch studded with diamonds and pearls. The balance is visible.

Bottom center.
Gold watch in a double case. Quarter hour repeater movement with verge escapement. Gold châtelaine with key and seal. Inner case pierced and engraved. Outer case repoussé with precious stones and cameo. Gold dial. Signature Joseph Wehrle.

Lower right.
Gold and enamel verge escapement watch in the form of a basket with handle. Swiss. Circa 1800.

Color Plate II.

Left.
Gold and enamel automaton watch. Quarter hour repeater. Figures on dial appear to be striking bells. Landscape painted on the back. Swiss. Circa 1830.

Center.
Enamelled musical box with watch in lid and surrounded by pearls. Swiss. Circa 1820.

Right.
Gold and enamel watch. Heavy gold outer case with a bezel on each side set with baroque pearls. Outer case decorated with a painted scene of family life. Enamel dial with gold hands and seconds hand. Signature William Ilbery. London. No. 6249. Circa 1800.

Color Plate III.

Top left.
A small enamelled striking watch with verge escapement. Enamel dial. Gilded, pierced and engraved case. Plate and dust cover signed Pe Dutens. London. No. 571. Circa 1750.

Top right.
Small gold and enamel watch. Plain gold dust cover. Gold outer case with enamel work on back. Front bezel studded with diamonds. Enamel dial with small diamonds on hand. Signature J's (Jacques) Patron. Genève. Circa 1770.

Bottom left.
Gold and enamel watch richly decorated with pearls. Gilt movement with duplex escapement. Enamel dial with small seconds hand. Signature Bovet. London. Circa 1840.

Bottom center.
Gold and enamel watch. Enamel dial with gilt hands. Signature G.H. (Guillaume Henri) Valentin à Genève. Circa 1780.

Bottom right.
Gold and enamel watch lavishly decorated with pearls.

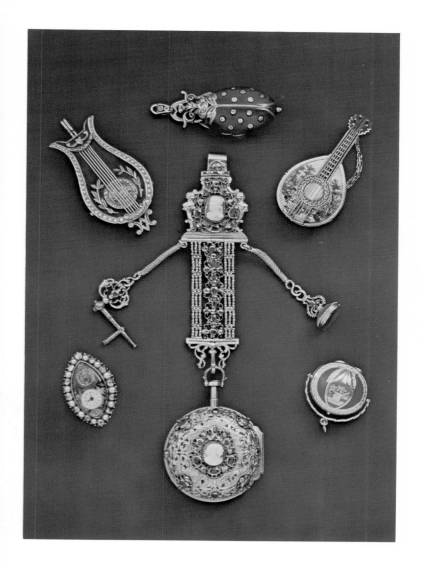

COLOR PLATE 1

COLOR PLATE 2

COLOR PLATE 3

The first real attempt by English makers to follow the French example came about 1830 when a few three-quarter plate movements were made. This involved cutting away part of the top plate to admit the balance and escape wheel and thereby reduce the overall thickness.

Near the end of the eighteenth century a few minute repeaters appeared. These struck the hour on the first bell, quarters on both bells, and the minutes on the second bell.

By this time clock-watches were being made that struck quarters as well as hours without selection on the part of the owner, and when a repeat mechanism was added it functioned also as a minute repeater.

A few watches are known to have been made with Grande Sonnerie but these are comparatively rare.

During the last quarter of the eighteenth century perpetual or self-winding watches began to appear.

Despite the advantages of fitting jewelled pivot holes, invented in 1704, and oil sinks, invented in 1715, watchmakers rarely used them before 1750. It was not until about 1775 that they came into general use.

By the end of the eighteenth century Harrison's maintaining power was in regular use and continued to be fitted to fusee watches until the end of the nineteenth century when the fusee was discontinued.

Escapements

The two most popular escapements remained the verge and the cylinder, described in Chapter One and Chapter Four respectively. The verge was used almost invariably in low-priced watches, while the majority of high quality watches were fitted with cylinder escapements despite the high rate of wear at the ends of the cylinder mouth. In the late eighteenth century, fitting ruby cylinders overcame this weakness.

In Switzerland, during the nineteenth century, the cylinder escapement was particularly popular. Very large numbers of thin watches were made with barred movements in which cylinder escapements were fitted.

It was inevitable that some of the many developments that took place during the evolution of the marine timekeeper should eventually be applied to watches. Two such applications were those of Arnold's pivoted detent and Earnshaw's spring detent, both of which began to appear in pocket watches about 1782.

Fig. 44a. An early 19th century French cylinder escapement watch. Engine turned silver dial with matt chapter ring and blued steel hands. Case is gold, engine turned all over and remarkably slim. Outer oval case of silver, engine turned all over. Diameter of watch 1¾ in. Signature Courvoisier & Cie. No. 5745.

Fig. 44b. The movement bridges are nickel, the plate is gilded, and the winding square is female.

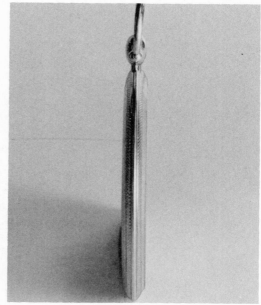

Fig. 44c. Side view showing the remarkable slimness. The thickest single part is the glass, just discernable on the right-hand side of the photograph.

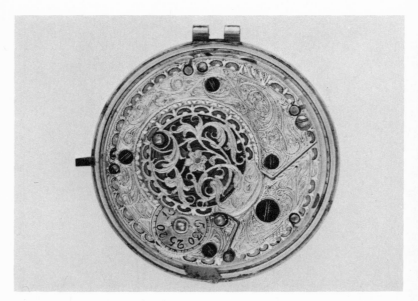

Fig. 45 Side view of an English cylinder escapement movement showing the hooked teeth of the escape wheel. Circa 1770.

FIG. 46. An English cylinder escapement movement showing the similarity to a verge watch of the same period. Diameter 1-7/16 in. Signature Ellicott. London. Circa 1765.

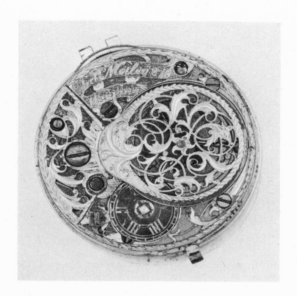

Fig. 47. A mid 18th century English verge escapement movement. Diameter 1⅜ in. Signature Richard Motley. Wapping (London). Circa 1765.

Fig. 48. Side view of an English cylinder escapement movement showing the hooked teeth of the escape wheel. Circa 1770.

Fig. 49. A late 18th century English cylinder escapement movement. Diameter 1⅜ in. Signature John Brockbank. London.

Fig. 50. A late 18th century English cylinder escapement movement showing dust cap which is also signed. Diameter 1¾ in. Signature John Kentish Junior. London. No. 1200.

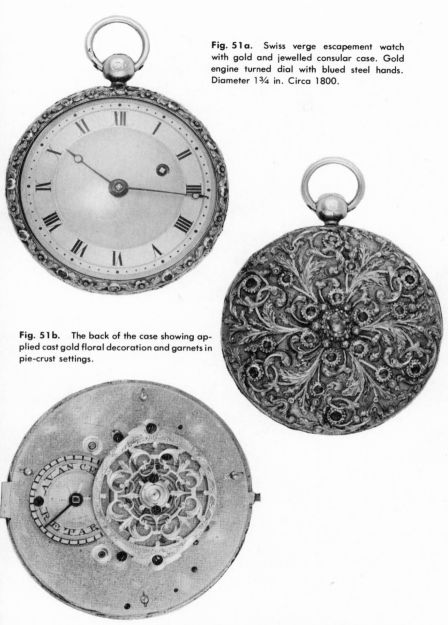

Fig. 51a. Swiss verge escapement watch with gold and jewelled consular case. Gold engine turned dial with blued steel hands. Diameter 1¾ in. Circa 1800.

Fig. 51b. The back of the case showing applied cast gold floral decoration and garnets in pie-crust settings.

Fig. 51c. The anonymous verge escapement movement.

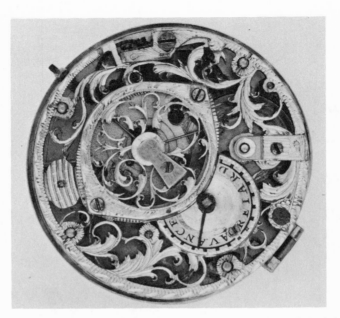

Fig. 52. A Swiss skeleton verge escapement movement. European-type balance bridge with two screws. Diameter 1¾ in. Anonymous. Circa 1800.

Fig. 53. An early 19th century English cylinder escapement movement. Verge escapement movements of this period look very similar. Diameter 1 9/16 in. Signature French. Royal Exchange. London.

Fig. 54a. The movement of an Earnshaw-type spring detent pocket chronometer. Note the Earnshaw balance. Diameter 2 in. Signature Charles John Cope, London. Circa 1815.

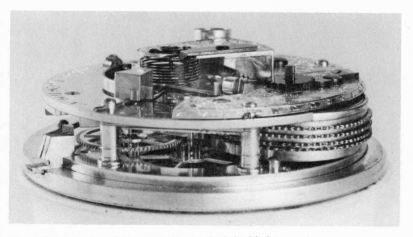

Fig. 54b. Side view of movement showing the helical balance spring.

Fig. 54c. Side view of movement showing the escape wheel, and on the left the detent block.

Fig. 55. An English rack lever escapement movement. This has a one way slide to adjust the depthing of the pallets. It is visible below the balance rim at the end of the balance cock. Diameter 1 15/16 in. Signature P. Litherland & Co. Liverpool. Circa 1799.

Fig. 56. English rack lever escapement movement. Note the use of a temperature compensation curb on the regulator index. Diameter 1¾ in. Signature Reid. Ball Alley. London. No. 6125. Circa 1835.

The rack lever and the Debaufre escapements (see Chapter Four) were rarely used during the eighteenth century until they were made popular by makers in the west of England. In 1791 Peter Litherland of Liverpool took out a patent covering the rack lever, and the escapement quickly enjoyed widespread popularity. The Debaufre escapement was made popular about 1800 by makers in the village of Ormskirk, near Liverpool, and it became generally known as the Ormskirk escapement.

In addition to those already mentioned, many new escapements were invented but the majority had no lasting effect on the develop-

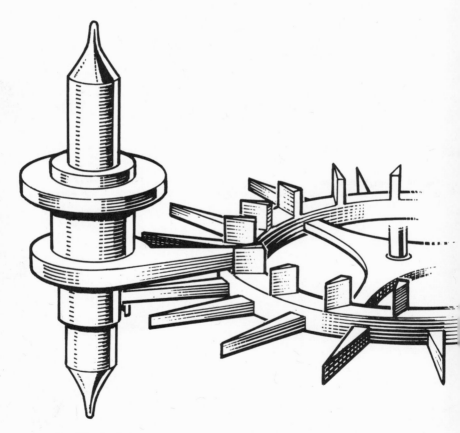

Fig. 57. Duplex escapement.

ment of the precision watch and are of little more than academic interest. Those with considerable influence over performance were the duplex and lever escapements.

Duplex Escapement

The duplex escapement, Fig. 57, was introduced by Pierre Le Roy in about 1750 but was never really popular in France. The French makers seemed to prefer Graham's cylinder presumably because it enabled them to produce thinner watches. The duplex enjoyed its greatest popularity in England during the first half of the nineteenth century, and of the many watchmakers who produced this form of escapement John McCabe made by far the greatest number.

The duplex was a frictional rest escapement. It was related to the cylinder escapement developed by Graham but had the distinct advantage of less friction. When made with care and precision it was capable of great accuracy and in high grade watches was frequently preferred to chronometer and lever escapements. The main disadvantage was its tendency to set because the impulse was given in one direction only.

The principle of operation can be seen in Figs. 58a and 58b. The escape wheel is cut with two sets of teeth: a horizontal set which are long and pointed, and a vertical set which are short and tapered. The horizontal teeth lock the escapement, and the vertical teeth give impulse to the balance.

In (a) one of the locking teeth is held against the side of the roller and the escape wheel is at rest. The balance staff is turning counter clockwise bringing the slot in the roller closer to the point of the locking tooth. The balance staff continues to rotate until the tooth enters the slot as shown at (b). The tooth is then able to escape the influence of the roller.

At the same time, the impulse pallet is positioned in the path of the oncoming impulse tooth; when the locking tooth escapes, the escape wheel turns causing the impulse tooth to push against the pallet and give impulse to the balance.

After the balance completes its swing it returns, and as the slot passes the tip of the succeeding locking tooth a slight recoil is produced.

It is usual for both sets of teeth to be cut on the same escape wheel but occasionally one finds a movement with two wheels, each with its own set of teeth, mounted one above the other on the same arbor. Such

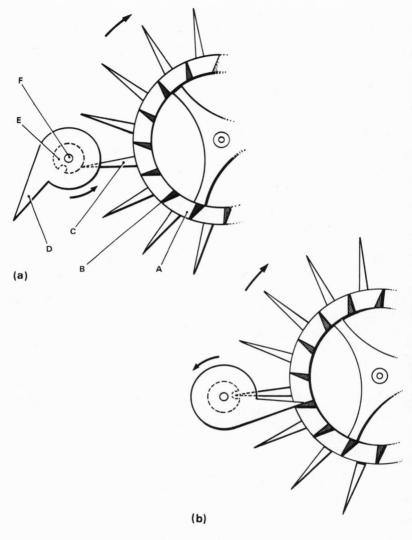

(a)

(b)

Fig. 58a. Operation of duplex escapement.

(A)	Escape wheel	(D)	Impulse pallet
(B)	Impulse tooth	(E)	Locking roller
(C)	Locking tooth	(F)	Balance staff

Fig. 58b. Operation of duplex escapement.

142

an arrangement is not uncommon in European watches. In late examples of this escapement the roller is frequently of ruby and the impulse face of the pallet is jewelled.

Lever Escapement

The escapements mentioned so far, with the exception of the chronometer detent, are all frictional rest escapements. That is to say the escape wheel teeth are continually in contact with the balance assembly, and friction occurs between them at each end of the swing in the supplementary arc. Watchmakers had for many years realized that a detached balance with complete freedom of movement would be capable of a superior performance.

It was not until 1754 that the first detached escapement was invented. Thomas Mudge had the brilliant idea of redesigning the Abbé de Hautefeuille's rack lever and dispensing with the rack and pinion. The result was a balance completely detached from the escapement except when an escape wheel tooth was unlocked or giving impulse.

The arrangement was referred to as Mudge's forked escapement. It did not become known as the lever escapement until after 1800.

It is generally accepted that the lever was an English invention, but recent evidence indicates that Julien Le Roy may well have had the idea of a detached lever at about the same time as Mudge.

Part of a watch movement was found among some junk in a stall on a Paris street. Only the escapement and the wheels are left but there are indications that it was originally fitted with temperature compensation. Inscribed round the edge of the plate are the words "Julien Le Roy Invenit et Fecit à Paris 4757." The number signifies that it was made during the last years of his life and, as he died in 1759, it is most likely that he ante-dated Mudge by a few years.

There is no evidence to show that Julien's son Pierre carried out any development of his father's idea. It is generally believed that it was Breguet who introduced the detached lever to France when he made the world-famous watch for Queen Marie-Antoinette in 1783.

Mudge spent most of his time on his marine timekeeper and paid little attention to the forked escapement. Had he pursued his idea a different story might now be told.

Mudge had every confidence in his invention. He once wrote ''I think, if well executed, it has great merit, and will, in a pocket watch particularly, answer the purpose of time-keeping better than any other at present known; yet it has the disadvantage that it requires great delicacy in execution that you will find very few artists equal to, and fewer still that will give themselves the trouble to arrive at; which takes much from its merit. And as to the honour of the invention, I must confess I am not at all solicitous about it; whoever would rob me of it does me honour.''

Mudge's lever watch is a beautiful piece of workmanship made for George III in 1759. It has a large gold pair-case with an enamel dial, blued steel poker and beetle hands and a center seconds hand. The king presented the watch to Queen Charlotte and to this day it has remained in the care of the royal family at Windsor Castle, England. It is known as the Queen's watch.

Count von Bruhl, a diplomat, was a friend of Mudge, and during the years that followed the completion of the Queen's watch, von Bruhl persistently tried to persuade Mudge to make a second lever watch, but always Mudge resisted. Eventually in 1782, at the age of sixty-seven, Mudge made for von Bruhl a rather rough model, and it is from this piece of workmanship that subsequent development of English lever watches was made.

Von Bruhl then persuaded Josiah Emery to make a pocket watch with an escapement exactly as Mudge's model. This he did and the watch was completed the same year.

It is not known for certain how many pocket lever watches were made by Emery but from the watch numbers, and the hallmarking dates, it seems he produced at least thirty-five, the last being in 1795. All the escapements were without draw. Of these watches only twelve are known to have survived, five are in British museums and the remaining seven are in private collections.

The first of Emery's watches had an escapement almost identical to Mudge's watch but then he changed the layout. Whereas Mudge's lever was aligned with the anchor, resulting in the pivots of the escape wheel, lever and balance forming a right angle, Emery arranged his lever at right angles with the anchor, and the three pivots formed a straight line. This arrangement contributed largely to producing a more vigorous action. Emery's layout was subsequently used extensively in Europe, but English makers, who generally followed Emery, reverted to the original arrangement as designed by Mudge.

Other English makers produced experimental lever watches in very limited numbers during the last fifteen years of the eighteenth century and it is doubtful whether more than about twenty-five watches have survived the pre-1800 period. Among the most prominent names are

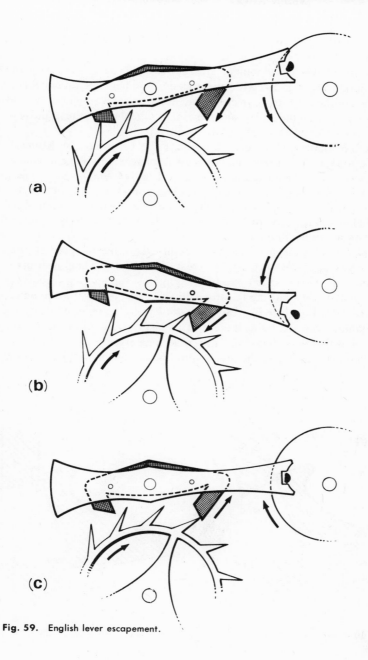

Fig. 59. English lever escapement.

Dutton, Ellicott, Grant, Leroux, Margetts, Pendleton, Perigal and Taylor.

From all this development emerged what is now known as the English lever, Fig. 59, with its pointed or ratchet-type escape wheel teeth. Unlike the European club tooth escapement where impulse was divided between the pallets and the escape wheel teeth, the impulse of an English lever was on the pallets only.

In the modern lever escapement all the essentials of Mudge's invention have been retained with few improvements. The one notable exception is the introduction of draw, Fig. 60, which was invented by John Leroux in 1785 but used by no other maker until after 1800.

Fig. 61 illustrates the escape wheel, the lever, two banking pins and the balance staff roller of a modern Swiss lever watch; the principle of operation can be studied in Fig. 62.

The escape wheel tooth hits the locking face of the entry pallet stone and the escape wheel is brought to rest, Fig. 62(a). The power in the escape wheel causes the tooth to press against the locking face of the entry pallet stone pulling the stone down. This downward movement is called the draw (see Fig. 60). The draw pulls the lever hard against the banking pin and holds it there. This last movement of the lever is known as the run to banking. If the watch received a shock sufficient to overcome the draw, the lever would no longer be held against the

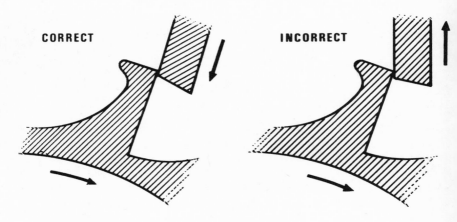

CORRECT   **INCORRECT**

Fig. 60. The draw.

banking pin and would be free to pass across to the other banking pin. This would cause the watch to stop. To prevent this from happening, a guard pin is fitted at the end of the lever which, under conditions described above, would come in contact with the roller and check further movement of the lever.

To allow the lever to pass under normal conditions the watchmaker cuts a groove in the edge of the roller level with the ruby pin.

The balance completes its swing, stops and reverses under the tension of the balance spring. The ruby pin enters the notch of the lever and moves the lever away from the banking pin. This causes the entry pallet stone to be pulled away from the escape wheel thereby releasing the tooth, Fig. 62, (b).

The ruby pin continues to move round pushing the lever farther over and the exit pallet stone moves in towards the escape wheel. The adjacent tooth strikes the exit pallet stone on its locking face and the lever is held firmly against the other banking pin, Fig. 62, (c).

The balance completes its swing and reverses direction. As the ruby pin re-enters the notch in the lever, the lever is moved away from the banking pin, pulling the exit pallet stone away from the escape wheel tooth. The escape wheel tooth, being freed from the locking face, now presses against the impulse face of the exit pallet stone. This impulse, transmitted through the lever, gives a further swing to the balance, Fig. 62, (d). While the exit pallet stone is being pushed away, the entry pallet stone is moving in to stop the next tooth and the cycle of operations repeats itself.

It remains a mystery why this escapement took so long to be accepted. Not until the end of the century was any real interest shown and still another fifty years passed before it became the most generally used form of escapement for quality watches. Because of its relative scarcity any lever watch made during the eighteenth century has considerable interest for any collector.

Virgule or Hook Escapement

The virgule, Fig. 63, was a frictional rest escapement and was a French development of the cylinder escapement. It derived its name from its similarity in shape to a comma. Jean-André Lepaute was the inventor but it was subsequently introduced by Jean Antoine about 1780. Its popularity in France was rapid but nevertheless short-lived; very few French watches are known to have been made with this escapement fitted after the opening years of the nineteenth century.

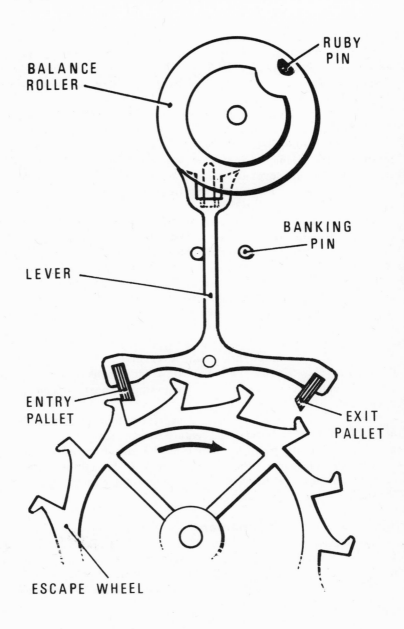

RUBY PIN

BALANCE ROLLER

BANKING PIN

LEVER

ENTRY PALLET

EXIT PALLET

ESCAPE WHEEL

Fig. 61. Modern lever escapement.

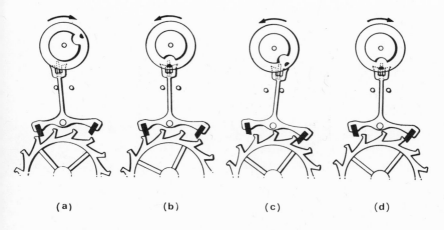

(a)　　　　　　(b)　　　　　　(c)　　　　　　(d)

Fig. 62. Operation of modern lever escapement.

The principal disadvantages were friction and the inability to retain oil.

Whereas in the cylinder escapement an impulse was created with each swing and was shared by the wheel and the cylinder, in the virgule an impulse was imparted at each alternate swing and was transmitted entirely to the cylinder.

The escape wheel teeth were tapered and the small outer ends were upstanding. In appearance they resembled the teeth of a cylinder escapement wheel with their toes removed.

In operation, Fig. 64, the escape wheel is halted by the oncoming tooth locking on the outer curved surface of the virgule, (a). Meanwhile the virgule rotates clockwise through an angle of approximately one hundred and eighty degrees bringing the entry pallet in line with the escape wheel tooth, (b), and allowing the tooth to enter, (c). The balance completes its clockwise swing and then reverses direction. The tooth can no longer be retained by the virgule and it is therefore allowed to escape. In so doing the tooth slides along the curved inner face of the exit pallet and delivers a strong impulse, (d). When the escaping tooth drops, (e), the following tooth moves forward and is arrested by the outer face of the virgule, (f). The virgule completes its counter clockwise swing, and the cycle is then repeated.

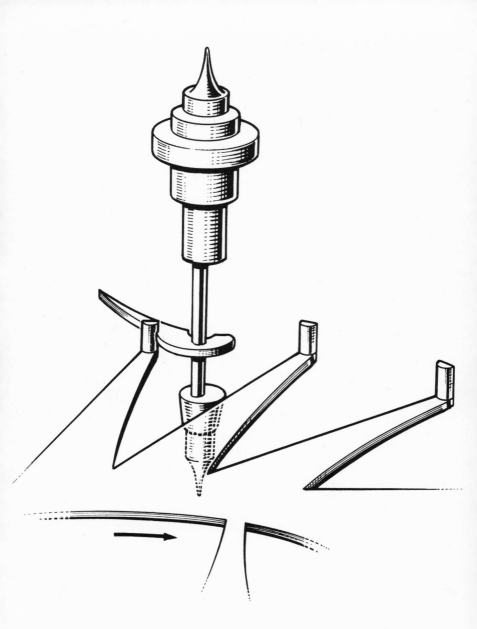

Fig. 63. Virgule escapement.

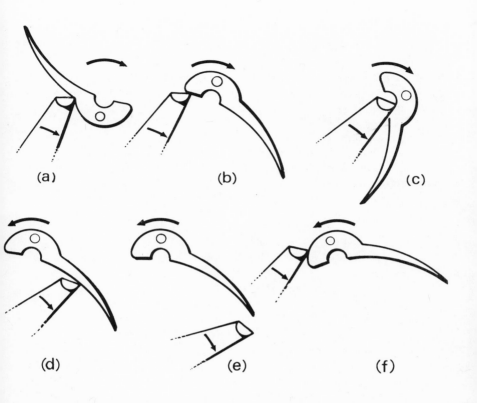

Fig. 64. Operation of virgule escapement.

Temperature Compensation

Sprung balances were very sensitive to changes in temperature. An increase caused a balance to expand and increased the diameter of the rim. This transferred the mass weight further from the central point of pivot and resulted in the balance swinging more slowly. The same rise in temperature also caused the balance spring to increase in length and lose some of its power. The combined effect was to slow the movement down.

A watch might well have operated during a winter's night in a room temperature of 40°F and in the morning have found itself in the waistcoat pocket of its owner snug in a temperature of 85°F. This rise of 45°F could well result in a loss in timekeeping of several minutes per day. Clearly, some form of temperature compensation was required.

Harrison was the first to attempt any form of temperature compensation in a watch when he fitted a riveted bimetallic compensation curb to his No. 3 marine timekeeper.

Then came the realization that any interference with an isochronous spring destroyed its isochronism, and makers turned to the balance to provide temperature compensation.

In 1766 Pierre Le Roy fitted a thermometer to a balance and found that the movement of mercury away from or closer to the center, when changes of temperature took place, altered the inertia of the balance and successfully cancelled any change in rate.

In 1770 Le Roy had the idea of a balance with a bimetallic rim but he preferred his thermometer and did not develop the new idea.

John Arnold in 1773 fitted a bimetallic spiral to a balance and arranged for two weights to move outward or inward during temperature changes by means of levers.

In 1778 Arnold fitted two straight bimetallic bars to his balances. This was followed in 1779 by two bimetallic S-shaped pieces fitted on opposite sides of the balance each connected to a movable weight. A rise in temperature caused the bimetallic pieces to pull the weights inward, and vice versa. In 1780 Arnold introduced balances with bimetallic rims. Each rim consisted of two laminated arms of brass and steel. The two metals were pre-shaped, the brass being on the outside, and then riveted together. A subsequent improvement in this method of assembly was to replace the rivets with soldering.

In 1782 Thomas Earnshaw introduced the far superior method of producing bimetallic rims by fusing together the two metals and thereby producing a completely homogeneous mass.

Earnshaw also introduced a compensation curb that became known as the ''sugar-tong.'' It consisted of two bimetallic arms fixed to the plate at one end and free to move at the other. At each free end was a pin and between the pins the balance spring was positioned. A change in temperature caused the gap between the arms to open or close and thereby alter the effective length of the spring.

Until about 1780 the majority of balances were steel but after that date brass balances with two, three or four arms quickly came into general use.

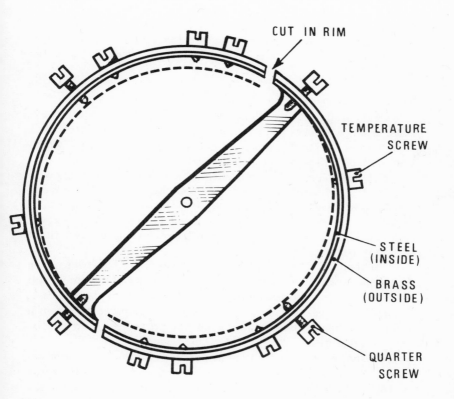

Fig. 65. Bimetallic compensation balance.

In 1787 Breguet fitted bimetallic balances to his watches and not long after their use became universal.

There are many designs of bimetallic balances among old watches but their basic principle of operation is the same. Fig. 65 illustrates a simple but more modern form. The four quarter screws, or timing screws as they are sometimes called, are adjusted to alter the timing. Turning two opposite screws outward slows down the watch and turning them inward speeds it up.

To supplement the action of the two rim arms during temperature changes the balance is supplied with a number of temperature screws. If a watch loses during rises in temperature these screws are removed and inserted in different holes nearer the free end of the arms. Positioning these screws further away from the free ends achieves the opposite effect.

Balance Springs

We have seen in Chapter Four that the earliest balance springs were fitted to verge watches and were made with one and a half turns. This soon became two to three turns, and occasionally four turns, which were enough to satisfy the requirement of a balance whose arc of swing was between one hundred and one hundred and twenty degrees. We also know that the cylinder escapement produced a wider arc and that it was necessary for the springs to be made with four to five turns.

When the lever escapement was invented the amount of swing was about one and three-quarters of a revolution and springs were fitted with ten or more turns.

Until about 1770 the quality of springs was poor. They were made from soft drawn wire and possessed very little elasticity. Being soft they were easily distorted and had to be handled with extreme care. Then came a steel that was capable of being tempered and from it springs were made that produced a much improved and more consistent performance.

The usual method of regulation was by Tompion's regulator described in Chapter Four but, in 1755, a new form of regulator was introduced by Joseph Bosley. This consisted of a pivoted lever which was positioned beneath the balance cock and moved concentrically with the balance arbor. The short arm of the lever carried two index pins that embraced the outer end of the balance spring and the long arm was moved across a scale engraved in the top plate. This form of regulator was little used until the turn of the century. It was the forerunner of the modern index.

Watchmakers were aware of isochronism and realized it was a property essential to a balance spring if timekeeping was to be improved.

When Arnold was working on his marine timekeepers he fitted helical springs and found by experiment that isochronism was obtained if one or both ends were curved inward (see Fig. 33, page 111).

Abraham-Louis Breguet adopted this idea and applied it to flat spiral springs by bending the outer coil up and over the volute (see Fig. 80, page 184). This design became known as the Breguet "overcoil" spring and is now used universally in good quality watches.

Isochronous springs are not usually fitted with regulators because their isochronism would be destroyed. Regulation is carried out before fitting and any subsequent adjustment is made by timing screws in the rim of the balance adjacent to the ends of the balance arms. Springs fitted in this way are referred to as "free-sprung."

Keyless Winding

The end of the eighteenth century saw the introduction of keyless winding to English watches and during the first quarter of the nineteenth century a variety of methods were used. All are known as pump winding because the action of winding the mainspring involves pulling out the pendant, or pushing it in, or both. But with all these types of keyless winding a key is still required to set the hands.

The earliest patent was taken out by Robert Leslie in 1793. In his design the mainspring was partially wound with each movement of the pendant.

In 1814 Edward Massey designed a push-wind for movements fitted with either a fusee or going barrel. After the pendant was depressed a spring returned it to its normal position.

Thomas Prest in 1820 introduced a form of pendant winding that was suitable only for going barrels. Almost all English watches at that time were fitted with fusees and so his idea was of little commercial value.

An unusual winding mechanism was developed by Joseph Berrollar in 1827. The cap of the pendant lifted off and attached to it was a length of chain similar to that used with a fusee. By pulling on the chain one wound the spring through a ratchet attached to the barrel arbor. When the cap was released the chain was pulled back into the watch and the process was repeated.

Cases

The movements of sixteenth century watches were hinged to their cases so they could be swung out for winding. It was not until after 1650 that winding holes were provided in dials and backs of cases. Even so, the practice of hinging movements and dial covers to cases continued into the third quarter of the nineteenth century, particularly among top class English watches.

Pair-cases remained popular in England until about 1890 but generally they were used for low-priced watches. The fashion for high grade watches changed to slimness about 1780 under the influence of

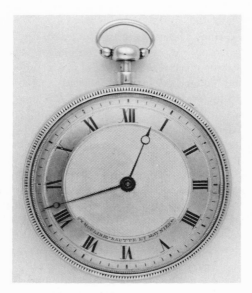

Fig. 66a. Swiss gold-cased quarter repeating watch with cylinder escapement. Gold engine turned dial and blued steel moon hands. Diameter 2¼ inches. Signature Moulinie, Bautte et Moynier. Circa 1820.

Fig. 66b. The movement showing the shock protecting parechute on the top balance pivot, and the temperature compensation curb on the regulator index. The influence of Abraham-Louis Breguet is evident.

Fig. 67. Gold one-minute tourbillon watch. Large hunter case with engine turned covers. The front bears a monogram M surmounted by a crown. Enamel dial with Roman hour numerals, Arabic ten-minute numerals, subsidiary dials for seconds and temperature, and blued steel moon hands. Gilt three-quarter plate movement with fusee, steel carriage, two-pin lever escapement, gold club tooth escape wheel, jewelled pallets and a bimetallic compensation balance. The escapement is fitted with a free-sprung spherical balance spring invented by the maker of the watch; Jacques Frédéric Houriet, Le Locle. Diameter 6.5 cm. Swiss. Circa 1815.

Fig. 68.

Top left.
Gold and enamel pair-cased quarter repeating verge watch. The back of the case is painted with a nativity scene, and the case band is decorated with bright-cut engraving. The inner case is pierced with arabesque designs. The movement has a pierced balance cock with a garnet endstone and is protected by a dust cover. Diameter 4.7 cm. Signature Soret & Fils, No. 6601. Circa 1780.

Top center.
Miniature gold and enamel cylinder watch. The back of the case is painted with a reclining maiden against a blue guilloché ground. Bezels are decorated with split pearls. Enamel dial with gold moon hands. Gilt and engraved movement. Diameter 2.5 cm. Signature Prior. Swiss. Circa 1790.

Top right.
Gold and enamel verge watch. The back of the case is painted with figures and inside is a landscape. The enamel dial is painted with Roman and Arabic numerals. The movement has a bridge balance cock and is signed L'Epine à Paris. Diameter 5.0 cm. Circa 1790.

Bottom left.
Gold and enamel verge watch. The case back is painted on the outside with a maiden playing a viol within a raised cartouche set with graduated split pearls. The border is painted with doves on a pale blue ground. Split pearls and engraving decorate the bezels. The movement dust cover and the dial are signed Fres Veigneur à Genève. No. 12804. Diameter 5.7 cm. Circa 1810.

Bottom center.
Gold and enamel châtelaine watch. Engraved case decorated in champlevé blue guilloché enamel enclosing an oval panel painted in grisaille with a classical subject. Gold mounted châtelaine en suite suspending two clips with matching heart locket and key. Enamel dial with Roman and Arabic numerals and diamond-set hands. Full plate movement with bridge balance cock. Quarter repeating. Cylinder escapement with gold escape wheel and diamond endstone. Dust cover signature Josiah Emery, London. No. 660. Circa 1775.

Bottom right.
Gold and enamel verge watch. Case in blue guilloché enamel and split pearls. Signature on dial and movement Chevalier & Compé, 4116. Diameter 5.2 cm. Swiss. Circa 1820.

Color Plate IV.

Top left.
Gold and enamel quarter repeater decorated with baroque pearls. Enamel dial with blued steel hands and center seconds hand. Circa 1800.

Top right.
Gold and enamel watch decorated with pearls and fitted with a cylinder escapement movement. Enamel dial, Roman numerals and blued steel hands. Swiss. Circa 1810.

Middle left.
Gold and enamel case heavily decorated with pearls. Finely engraved duplex escapement movement. London. Circa 1790.

Middle right.
Gold and enamel watch with pearl decoration. Enamel dial with small seconds hand. Signature Barrauds. London. No. 9673. Circa 1820.

Bottom left.
Gold and enamel case set with baroque pearls. Enamel dial with blued steel hands and small seconds hand. Swiss. Circa 1800.

Bottom right.
Gold and enamel case decorated with pearls. Enamel dial with Arabic figures and gold hands. Verge escapement movement. Signature F's Veigneur à Genève. No. 12084. Circa 1790.

Color Plate V

Top left.
Gold case enamelled inside and outside. Gold dial with Arabic and Roman numerals. In the center is a victory angel with wreath. Verge escapement movement. Signature Tho. Tompion. London. Circa 1710.

Center.
Gold and enamel astronomical watch. Case set with pearls and gems. Enamel dial with subsidiary dials for days, date, month and moon phase. Signature F.L. Godon. Rio de Camara de S.M.C.

Top right.
Montre à tact with flat gold guilloché case. Tact decorated with diamonds. Cylinder escapement movement. Signature Breguet 608. Circa 1800.

Lower left.
Gold and enamel case in the form of a harp, decorated with diamonds and pearls. Probably Swiss. Circa 1810.

Lower right.
Gold case. The kitchen scene on the back is in multi-colored gold and enamel. The dial is enamel with gold hands. The movement has a cylinder escapement.

Bottom.
Gold pistol-shaped watch decorated with pearls. Pressing the trigger sprays perfume from the barrel. Swiss. Circa 1800.

COLOR PLATE 4

COLOR PLATE 5

French makers who were then developing watches of greatly reduced thickness. In European watches enamelling no longer completely covered the outside of the case but instead was confined to a panel on the back. Around the panel the case was frequently decorated with repoussé, or was pierced for repeaters and clock-watches, while gems or half-pearls were applied to the edge. Repoussé showed a marked decline in quality after 1750 and by 1770 it had almost disappeared.

The majority of good quality English watches had cases of silver or gold which were either plain with no form of decoration or were decorated on the backs with engine turning. Many of the cheaper watches had cases made of transparent horn. The insides were painted with pictures of butterflies and flowers, so, though inexpensively produced, the watches were nevertheless very attractive.

Goldsmiths discovered that, by mixing with alloys, they could tint gold green, yellow, red and silvery-white. This form of case decoration was used in Europe very occasionally during the second half of the eighteenth century, but after 1800 it became very popular both in Europe and in England. It is referred to as four-color gold and was generally used in conjunction with repoussé and pierced work. Tinted gold was in regular use up to about 1875 and was particularly popular in Switzerland.

Form watches became popular again in Switzerland early in the nineteenth century and have remained so ever since.

Pendants

During the second half of the eighteenth century the fashion for pendant bows slowly changed from the stirrup type back to the oval shape of the seventeenth century. Then, after 1800, they changed to the plain round ring which has since been universally adopted. Repeat mechanisms were designed to be operated by depressing the pendant and so the necks had to be longer than usual. This however does not mean that a watch with a long pendant neck is necessarily a repeater.

Dials and Hands

During the first half of the eighteenth century gold and silver dials enjoyed considerable popularity in England, and then, about 1750, white enamel dials began to increase in number until, by about 1780, very few gold or silver dials were made. There was a transition period during which the very best watches had dials of gold that were coated

Fig. 69.

Top left.
Gold and enamel plum-shaped form watch. Movement signature J. Et. Pior, No. 8590.
Swiss. Circa 1820.

Top center.
Gold and enamel fruit-shaped form watch. Enamel dial signed Maurissot à Genève. Swiss.
Circa 1830.

Top right.
Gold and enamel stag-beetle form watch. Beetle black enamel and gold, with split
pearl-set legs, mounted on a green enamel oak leaf. The back legs open the wings to reveal
a verge watch. Swiss. Circa 1800.

Middle left.
Gold and enamel mandolin form watch. Round board of red guilloché enamel within split
pearl border. Black enamel neck and gold wire strings. Musical scene on back within a
black frame containing a cylinder watch. Swiss. Circa 1820.

Middle center.
Gold and enamel jockey cap form watch. The gold, red and blue cap is hinged to reveal a
cylinder watch. Signature L. Doring. Leipzig. Circa 1850.

Middle right.
Gold and enamel beetle form watch. Engraved gold body with ruby eyes and diamond set
thorax. The wings are red with black spots and open to expose the watch. Swiss. 20th
century.

Bottom left.
Gold and enamel scent bottle form watch. The bottle is black and gold and is suspended by
two chains attached to a finger ring. Swiss. Circa 1830.

Bottom center.
Gold and enamel harp form watch. Curved neck decorated with red, white and green
chevrons. Engraved gold musical trophies mounted on the enamelled sound box which is
hinged to reveal a verge watch. Swiss. Early 19th century.

Bottom right.
Gold and enamel flower basket form watch. Enamel flowers and split pearl basket. Swiss.
Circa 1830.

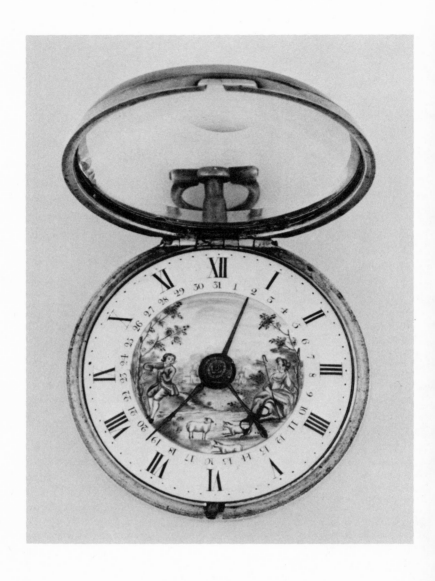

Fig. 70. Painted enamel dial of a late 18th century "Farmer's" verge escapement watch. The rustic scene was often applied to cheaper rather coarse verge watches of this period and later. This one is unusual in having a central calendar hand. Diameter 1¾ in.

164

with white enamel but even this was discontinued before the end of the century.

The most usual marking on European and English white enamel dials during the middle of the eighteenth century consisted of a circle outside of which were Roman hour numerals, then a double circle containing the minute divisions, and finally the minute numerals in Arabic at five-minute intervals. These minute numerals were in regular use until about 1770, but after that date they were used less frequently until by the end of the century they had almost disappeared.

Arabic hour numerals began to appear about 1770 but Roman figures remained the fashion. The innermost circle on the dial was usual until about 1790 and then it fell into disuse.

Subsidiary dials for date, month, up-and-down indicator, equation work, temperature, moon phase and seconds became more frequent, but the practice of recessing the subsidiary dials by grinding away the enamel was not introduced until after 1850.

Enamel dials were frequently provided with a round keyhole through which the movement was wound but this was not a good design. The presence of the hole spoiled the appearance of the dial and in many instances took away half of one of the numerals. The continual insertion of the key damaged the enamel which cracked and became degraded.

Among the more expensive English watches that appeared in the early years of the nineteenth century were those with a dial of four-color gold. The dial plate was engine turned from gold of one color, and highly polished skeleton numerals of another color were applied by solder. Outside the chapter ring the dial was decorated with floral designs in the remaining two colors.

Some of the most elegant dials were finished in matt yellow gold with applied polished numerals and blued steel or polished gold serpentine (wavy) hands.

Early nineteenth century European watches of quality were invariably fitted with a gold or silver dial decorated in the center with chased figures in a classical setting surrounded by an enamelled chapter ring. Cheap novelty watches with painted dials were very popular. Sometimes the painting extended to the edge of the dial plate and the dial proper occupied a space in the center. Another variation was to completely cover the dial plate with the picture and introduce the dial proper as the principal detail of the scene such as a church clock. An additional novelty was the use of automata such as the rocking of a

165

boat, the rotation of the sails of a windmill or figures passing across an opening. If the watch was fitted with a repeat mechanism the automata were usually arranged to move coincidentally with each strike. Sometimes a small slide was provided which, when moved to one side, revealed two figures engaged in amorous activity.

The use of beetle and poker hands in polished gold or blued steel was universal until John Arnold introduced his simple spade-ended hour hand about 1780. Beetle and poker hands then began to disappear and were rarely seen after 1800.

Form Watches

As was previously mentioned, after going out of fashion about 1665, form watches returned shortly after 1800 as a new fashion for women. The majority were produced in Switzerland and were designed in an ever increasing variety of shapes for brooch or chain suspension. Their popularity continued and today they represent a large part of the Swiss export market.

Watches for Chinese and Turkish Markets

During the latter part of the eighteenth century, watches for the Chinese market were made in Switzerland and in England but after 1800 the Swiss monopolized this export business. The cases were lavishly decorated with applied brilliants on enamel. Movement plates and bridge pieces were decorated with engine turning or intricate engraved designs, and balance wheels carried ''eyes'' to frighten evil spirits away. The dials were enamelled and many carried a center seconds hand that jumped forward at each second. Curiously enough these Swiss watches were frequently made in pairs.

Towards the end of the eighteenth century and during the first quarter of the nineteenth century a great many pocket watches were made in England for export to Turkey. At the same time, but to a much lesser extent, watchmakers in France were doing the same thing. The watches were typical of the period in which they were made, the only obvious difference being the Turkish numerals on the dial.

CHAPTER 7
Supremacy Returns to France
(1770-1830)

IN 1657 Christiaan Huygens invented the clock pendulum. In 1671 William Clement introduced Dr. Robert Hooke's invention of the anchor escapement for clocks. In 1672 Hooke invented the wheelcutting machine. Then, in 1675 came another invention from Huygens, the balance spring for watches.

Aided by these new ideas, and his own genius, Thomas Tompion produced clocks and watches that maintained a degree of accuracy never before achieved. Almost immediately the French lost their supremacy and the English became foremost in the field of horology, a position they held for over a century.

To conclude the story in this book we must now focus our attention on France, and in particular on Abraham-Louis Breguet.

Throughout the eighteenth century the English continued to concentrate on mechanical improvements with little regard to fashion. About 1782 Breguet, who was in Paris, began developing a new style of watch. He lived to become the most eminent maker in France during his time but not as the result of his unquestionable mechanical skill; his watches were no better timekeepers than those of other eminent makers. Breguet's triumph was in his natural ability to produce watches of great elegance and beauty. His taste and sense of proportion were impeccable. His artistry revolutionized fashion among pocket watches and regained for France the supremacy she had lost.

Breguet was born in Neuchâtel, Switzerland, in 1747, and was apprenticed to a watchmaker in Versailles, France, in 1762. Little is

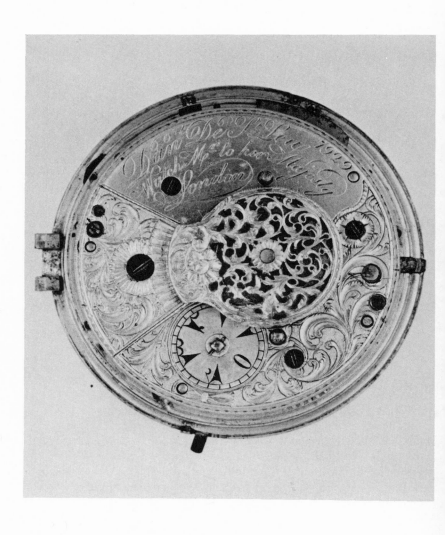

Fig. 71. The movement of a quarter striking verge escapement clock-watch for the Turkish market. Note the two winding squares, one on either side of the balance cock. Diameter 1½ in. Signature Daniel de St. Leu. London. Circa 1770.

Fig. 72a. A triple cased verge escapement watch for the Turkish market. Diameter 3⅛ in. Signature Isaac Rogers. London. No. 19043. Hallmark, London 1792.

Fig. 72b. The back of the shagreen-covered case showing the silver piqué work.

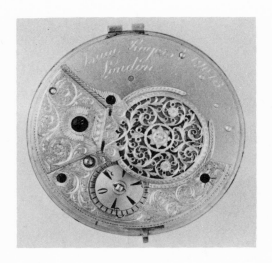

Fig. 72c. The verge escapement movement.

Fig. 72d. Inside the middle case showing the original watch paper.

Fig. 73a. A triple cased verge escapement watch for the Turkish market. White enamel dial with blued steel beetle and poker hands. Diameter 2⅜ in. Signature Edward Prior, London. Circa 1800.

Fig. 73b. The outer shell-covered case with silver piqué work.

Fig. 73c. The back of the second silver case showing the high standard of the engraved decoration.

Fig. 73d. The movement.

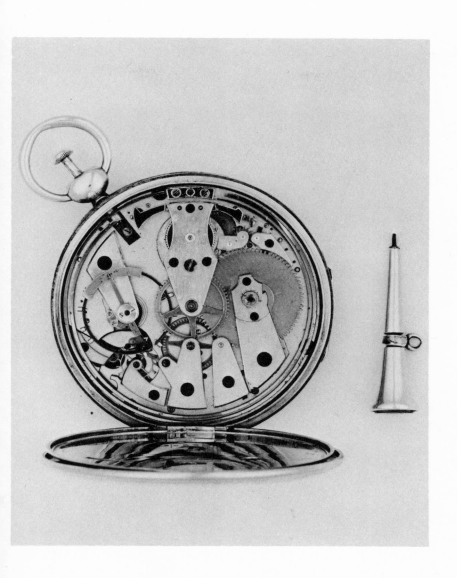

Fig. 74. A French half and quarter repeating watch movement. Straight line lever escapement with bimetallic compensation balance. Original male key. Diameter 2-1/16 in. Signature Blondeau. Paris. Circa 1835.

Fig. 75. Equation watch with date and month. Strike mechanism. Diameter 5.5 cm. Signature Lépine.

Fig. 76a. Swiss gold-cased cylinder escapement watch with silver engine turned dial and gold moon hands. Diamater 1¾ in. Signature Robert Melly et Cie. à Genève. No. 2020. Circa 1820.

Fig. 76b. The Lepine caliber movement of the watch.

known about the first forty years of his life. It is believed he worked for Ferdinand Berthoud until about 1782 and then went into business on his own. In 1787 the firm of Breguet started keeping business records and since then has maintained their books continuously. It has therefore not been too difficult for historians to follow the progress of Breguet from 1787 until he died in 1823.

Early Cylinder Watches

The earliest Breguet watch known to exist is No. 2 10/82. This method of fractional numbering was used by Breguet on all his early watches. No. 2 is the serial number and the fraction is the date; in this instance the fraction signifies that the watch was made in October 1782. It is a self-winding watch with cylinder escapement which once belonged to Marie-Antoinette. Engraved on the case is the inscription "Inventé, perfectionné et exécuté par Breguet" and "Breguet à Paris No. 2 10/82." The signature "Breguet à Paris" is to be found on all Breguet watches up to about 1793. A watch bearing this signature after 1795 is almost certain to be a fake and needs to be scrutinized closely.

Early Lever Watches

Breguet was the first European maker to use the lever escapement. His interest began about 1786 and he started making lever watches using the straight line arrangement favored by Emery.

Perpétuelles (Self-Winding Watches)

The first thirty watches to be recorded in the Breguet books were all quarter repeater "perpétuelles" with lever escapements. This type of watch had a thin bimetallic compensation balance and helical steel balance spring with end curves and regulator. The dial was enamel with subsidiary dials for seconds and up-and-down indication. There was no provision for key winding.

The movement was fitted with two going barrels that were wound, through a ratchet, by a pivoted platinum weight that swung as the wearer moved. The amount the springs were wound was shown on the up-and-down subsidiary dial. Stop work prevented the weight from swinging when the springs were fully wound.

The cases, dial markings and hands were exquisitely proportioned and their elegance heralded the arrival of a new style that was destined to take the lead in watch design. With these, now famous, watches

Breguet established himself as an artist among makers.

In addition to his pre-1787 cylinder watches, Breguet made two hundred and ninety-five watches by 1793. Then came the French Revolution and it was not long before he lived in fear for his life. He fled the country, first to Switzerland and then to England where he remained until 1795 when it was safe for him to return.

Secret Signature

As soon as Breguet arrived back in Paris he set to work rebuilding his business. He quickly discovered that during his absence other makers had been forging his signature on their own watches and so he devised a secret signature.

By means of a diamond pointed pantograph he reproduced his signature in miniature at the top of each dial. The signature is about one eighth of an inch long and one thirty-second of an inch high.

On enamel dials the signature, together with the number of the watch, appears below the numeral 12 and above the dial fixing screw. It is very faint and needs to be viewed across the dial against a strong light before it becomes visible.

On metal dials the signature appears twice: between XI and XII, and again between XII and I. The watch number does not always accompany the signature. On the majority of silver dials it is not possible to see the signature. Silver tarnishes readily and any attempt to restore the finish invariably removes the already shallow signature. It therefore follows that although the presence of a secret signature is reasonable evidence that the watch is a genuine Breguet, it does not follow that the absence of his signature is necessarily an indication that the watch is a fake.

Lepine Caliber

About 1770 Jean Antoine Lepine introduced a completely new form of movement. He dispensed with the use of a top plate with the balance mounted on the outside and located the upper pivots of the train, including the balance, in separate cocks or bars screwed to the bottom plate. He then removed the fusee and employed a going barrel thereby producing a movement of considerably reduced thickness.

Apart from his very early work, Breguet almost invariably used the Lepine caliber and it was his adaptation of Lepine's invention that enabled him to produce his famous slim watches.

Ruby Cylinder Escapement

Breguet was well aware of the improved performance produced by lever and detent escapements but even so, from the beginning of the nineteenth century, the majority of his watches were fitted with cylinder escapements. He considered that a disadvantage of Graham's cylinder escapement was the fragility of the balance staff caused by the cut-away portion of the cylinder (see Fig. 13, page 62). This weakness was aggravated by the relatively high cost of producing a replacement staff. Breguet overcame this by redesigning the staff as shown in Fig. 77. He increased the diameter to allow for an extension. Attached to the end of the extension was a U-shaped cylinder to which was cemented a ruby cylinder of the same shape. The lower pivot of the balance staff was located in a potence screwed to the movement plate. The ruby projected through the plate to engage the escape wheel situated beneath the dial. A feature on most Breguet watches was that the dial had to be removed to expose the escapement. The modified design had the desired effect of increasing the escapement's resistance to breakage from shock or mishandling.

Balances were usually plain and made of gold; it was more usual to fit compensation balances to lever and detent escapements. Flat spiral balance springs were used in conjunction with a regulator, and Bre-

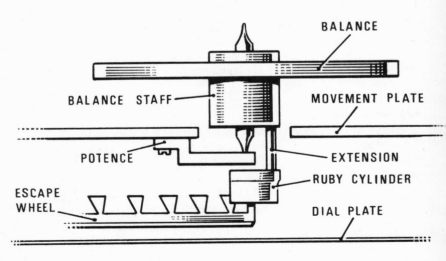

Fig. 77. Abraham-Louis Breguet's ruby cylinder escapement.

Fig. 78.

Left.

Gold watch by Breguet. White enamel dial with secret signature. Eccentric chapter ring above with a subsidiary dial for date below. Moon hands. Lever escapement with compensation balance and Breguet spring. Diameter 4.0 cm. Signature Breguet. No. 4684.

Center.

Gold regulator dial watch by Le Roy. Slim engine turned case. Gilt L'Epine caliber movement with cylinder escapement and plain balance. Engine turned silver dial with hour aperture at 12 o'clock. Eccentric minute ring and subsidiary seconds. Signature on gold cuvette; Le Roy, Palais Royal, No. 114. Diameter 5.2 cm. French. Circa 1820.

Right.

Gold watch by Breguet. Ruby cylinder escapement with parechute. Guilloché silver dial. Diameter 3.9 cm. Signature Breguet. No. 4419. Circa 1826.

guet applied his own form of compensation curb. This consisted of a regulator to which was fixed a pin and a U-shaped bimetallic strip. The free end of the bimetallic strip also carried a pin and passing between the two pins was the spring. A change in temperature caused the free end of the strip to move varying the distance between the two pins and thus altering the effective length of the balance spring. The fixed pin and the curb were both mounted on the regulator so that they moved together when regulating for mean time.

Since there was no fusee in the Lepine caliber Breguet used the largest diameter possible for his going barrels. He then restricted the going period to the middle of the spring in order to achieve a force of constant torque. It was the fitting of large diameter barrels that caused some watch dials to have an eccentric chapter ring.

About this time circular wire gongs began to be used in place of bells in repeat watches. The gongs took up less space and were well suited to the slim watches being introduced by Breguet.

The general arrangement of Breguet's cylinder watches was very successful, and the ruby cylinder reduced wear to such an extent that surviving watches work equally well today.

Tipsy Key

In 1789 Breguet introduced his ratchet winding key. It was made in two sections separated by a spring-loaded ratchet that ensured winding in one direction only. Its function was to prevent damage to the movement in the event that the key was turned in the wrong direction. It is generally referred to as the "tipsy key."

Parechute

In 1790 Breguet invented a form of shock absorber that he called his "parechute." It was designed to protect the upper pointed pivot of the balance staff from damage caused by shock. To the balance cock he screwed a long slender piece of thin spring steel, and in the free end of the spring he fitted the jewel hole and endstone. The tension of the spring was sufficient to hold the balance under normal wearing conditions, and if the watch was dropped, or otherwise subjected to shock, the resilience of the spring would allow the shock to be absorbed and the balance would then be returned to its normal functional position without damage to the top pivot.

When conical pivots were used a similar spring was screwed to the bottom plate to protect the lower pivot.

The Famous Marie-Antoinette Watch

Shortly before the outbreak of the French Revolution Breguet made his first perpetual calendar mechanism. It was fitted to a watch that had been ordered in 1783 for Queen Marie-Antoinette and was eventually finished in 1800. It is probably the most famous watch in the world after the Queens Watch made by the Englishman Thomas Mudge in 1770.

The movement is made of gold and steel, and is fully jewelled and rollered. It has a lever escapement with bimetallic compensation balance and helical spring. Its complicated work consists of perpetual calendar, self-winding mechanism with up-and-down indicator, minute repeater, equation of time, independent seconds and thermometer. The number is 160. Breguet was the first European maker to employ the use of jewels.

Montres à Répétition

The majority of Breguet's repeaters, "montres à répétition," are fitted with a cylinder escapement and compensation curb. Strike is made either on a wire gong or a metal block, and the push-piece is mounted on the side of the case or positioned in the neck of the pendant. Many have an unusual arrangement whereby the hour hand remains stationary for an hour and then, at each hour, jumps to the next numeral. It is referred to as a "jump hour hand."

Regulateur à Tourbillon

The rate of a watch will vary depending on its position, e.g. dial up, dial down, 9 up, 12 up and 3 up. To eliminate this by regulation requires complex adjustments to balance and balance spring which are tedious and lengthy and by no means lasting.

To a great extent Breguet reduced this variation in rate by eliminating the errors that occur in the vertical positions. This he did by designing his "regulateur à tourbillon."

The tourbillon was an arrangement whereby the escape wheel, lever or spring detent, and balance were all mounted on a revolving platform that was fixed to the fourth wheel arbor, Fig. 79. The third wheel drove the fourth wheel pinion which turned the platform by means of the fourth wheel arbor. The fourth wheel was fixed by screws to the bottom plate and the arbor passed freely through its center.

When the platform rotated, the escape wheel pinion was made to roll round the fourth wheel causing the pinion to rotate and thereby drive the escape wheel.

Since this arrangement caused the escapement to rotate a full circle when the watch was in the vertical position, all vertical position errors occurred and thus canceled one another.

The speed at which the platform rotated was determined by the layout of the movement. The early tourbillons rotated once in every minute. With such an arrangement it was convenient to extend the fourth wheel arbor through the dial to drive a seconds hand. Breguet then discovered that the inertia required to start the platform at each oscillation of the balance required a more powerful mainspring. He overcame this problem by altering the gear ratio to produce speeds of four and five minutes for each revolution. This he did by fixing the fourth wheel to the platform.

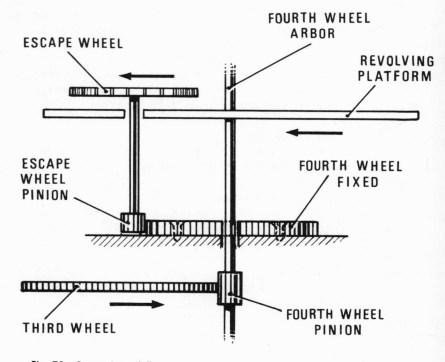

Fig. 79. Breguet's tourbillon.

The skill required in making a tourbillon was such that no other maker in Breguet's time would consider the task.

Montres à Tact

In 1796 Breguet introduced his "montre à tact." It was intended as an aid to determining the time in darkness and not as a watch specifically for the blind. The tact was a stout steel hand that pivoted on the center of the back of the case. Around the edge of the case were twelve touch pieces fixed at the hour positions. Attached to the center wheel of the movement was a ratchet with one tooth that engaged with a catch on the tact. If the tact was rotated counter clockwise the catch over-rode the ratchet tooth, but if the tact was turned clockwise, rotation was possible only until the catch met the ratchet tooth in which position further rotation was prevented. The tact was then pointing to the correct time which the wearer determined by feeling the position of the tact in relation to the touch pieces.

It is evident that any attempt to hold the tact would have no effect on the running of the movement; it was therefore quite safe to wear in the pocket.

On these watches the touch pieces and the tact were frequently embellished with pearls or diamonds, such decoration being a departure from Breguet's normal practice of artistic control.

Montres Mixtes

The "montres mixtes," though bearing genuine Breguet signatures, were nevertheless not made in his workshop, are not recorded in the Breguet books, and cannot be given a certificate.

They were usually high grade watches that were made under Breguet's supervision and then taken to his establishment for regulation and final inspection.

It is not possible to distinguish them from a genuine Breguet except by the secret signature "Breguet et Mixte."

Overcoil Balance Spring

Breguet's detent watches were fitted with free-sprung helical balance springs and fusees and were specifically made for timekeeping accuracy; there was no pretense at producing a slim watch. In other watches, where slimness was required, Breguet fitted flat spiral balance springs. He found by experiment that Arnold's method of producing isochronism, bending inward the two end coils of a helical

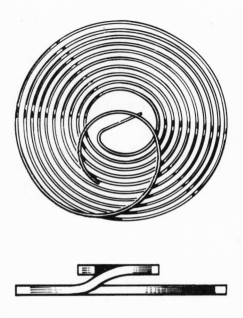

Fig. 80. Breguet's flat spiral balance spring with overcoil.

spring, applied equally well to a flat spiral spring. This new form of balance spring became known as Breguet's overcoil, Fig. 80, and is in regular use to this day.

Duplex Escapement

Very occasionally, after 1800, Breguet used the duplex escapement but always in high class watches. He arranged to have two wheels, one of gold to take the impulse action and the other of steel for the locking action.

Montres à Souscription

Breguet offered the public good quality watches made to a simple design at low cost, ''montres à souscription.'' To make this possible he needed to manufacture them in batches and so he asked for part payment in advance when ordering the watch.

The movement included a ruby cylinder escapement with a plain gold balance and spiral steel balance spring, regulator, "parechute," and going barrel that contained a large powerful spring.

The diameter of the dial was 2 5/16 inches and between each pair of hour numerals were twelve divisions, each one representing five minutes. There was only an hour hand but the length of each division was large enough to make possible the reading of time to within one to two minutes. The owner wound the watch through the center of the hand and had to push the hand round manually to set the time. The dials were enamel or gold with a blued steel hand. Occasionally a silver dial was used together with a gold hand.

The body of the case was silver and flat-sided. The glass was held by a gold snap-on bezel, and the back was a snap-on type made of silver and either decorated with engine turning or left plain. The pendant ring was loose fitting and made of gold.

These watches carried a secret signature consisting of the word "souscription," followed by the number of the watch and then "Breguet."

Cases

Rather than swing the movement out of its case for winding, as with English watches, and expose the movement to dirt and dust, French makers arranged for the winding key to be inserted in a hole cut in the dial. The edge of the hole eventually chipped and cracked and the appearance of the dial was spoiled.

Breguet introduced a different arrangement. He secured the movement to the inside of the annular body of the case, and to the outside he hinged a bezel at the front, and a movement cover or cuvette and a bezel at the rear. The front bezel held the rock crystal or glass, the cuvette snapped shut over the movement, and the rear bezel held the back of the case. The owner wound the watch by opening the back and inserting a key into a hole in the cuvette.

The only extraneous decoration that Breguet would countenance on his watch cases was that previously described for his "montres à tact," and enamel work for his large export of watches to Turkey. Case decoration was otherwise restricted to engine turning with possibly the addition of a heraldic cartouche on the back which was protected by transparent enamel.

Dials and Hands

Almost without exception enamel dials on Breguet watches were painted with sloping Arabic numerals, so the presence of Roman numerals should arouse suspicion; the watch may be a fake. Enamel dials were held by one screw just below the 12.

Seconds subsidiary dials were not usual on enamel. When they were present, however, they were likely to be anywhere on the dial depending on the layout of the movement.

Metal dials were introduced at the beginning of the nineteenth century and, almost invariably, Roman numerals were used for the hour markings.

Seconds subsidiary dials were more frequent on metal dials and it was normal for them to be recessed in the dial plate.

Breguet standardized the design of his watch hands. They were long and slender, and near the outer end was an eccentric ring typifying the moon; they became known as moon hands.

Dating a Watch

When Breguet started his own business in 1782 he serial numbered his watches using the fractional method previously described. This series of numbers was discontinued in 1788.

In 1787, when the Breguet books were started, a new series was used but without the fractional content. By the outbreak of the Revolution the numbering had reached 295. After the Revolution, when Breguet returned to Paris, he continued with the numbering until his death in 1823 by which time the numbering had reached 4,000.

It was quite usual for Breguet to buy back his watches, modernize them, and resell them with a higher number. Collectors know instances of this happening more than once to the same watch. It therefore follows that a watch could be earlier than its number suggests.

The following table gives some idea of the relationship between numbers and dates.

Serial Number	Year
295	1793
500	1800
1000	1803
2000	1809
3000	1818
3500	1820
4000	1823

Fig. 81a. A French quarter repeating watch with cylinder escapement, parechute and temperature compensation curb. Diameter 2 1/16 in. Circa 1820.

Fig. 81. The gilt cuvette showing the fake signature.

A further aid to determining the age of a Breguet watch is the signature. All watches are signed on the movement plate and on the dial outside the minute ring at the 6 o'clock position. Until 1795 the signature was "Breguet à Paris" but after that date it was changed to "Breguet." In about 1807 Breguet's son joined his father in partnership and the signature was then changed to "Breguet et Fils."

In 1815 the honor of being appointed "Horloger de la Marine" was conferred upon Breguet and the appointment was frequently engraved on the case cuvette.

After Breguet's death, and for a short period only, some watches were signed "Breguet et Neveu."

A watch bearing a signature with an accent, "Bréguet," is almost certainly a fake, Fig. 81b.

Many of Breguet's apprentices subsequently set up their own business and, in the majority of instances, their signature is the only indication that their work is not that of their master. Among these men were the following:

John Roger Arnold	Kessels
(son of John Arnold)	Laissieur
Frederick Louis Fatton	Lopin
Firche	Charles Oudin
Pierre-Frédérick Ingold	Renevier
Jacob	Winnerl
Urban Jürgensen	Michel Weber

They were extraordinarily well trained and considered it an honor to be able to sign their work linking their name with that of the man who is regarded by many as the most eminent of all horologists. Their signatures are followed by the words "élève de Breguet."

Watches made by Breguet are constantly being sought by collectors and when one is acquired it competes for top place in any collection.

CHAPTER 8
Styles of Decoration

Piercing

The gilt metal cases of the earliest watches were invariably cast in open work arabesque designs. The open work, or piercing as it is generally known, was necessary to release the sound of the alarm or strike bell, but it did nothing to safeguard the cleanliness of the movement. This method of decorating the cases continued well into the eighteenth century, but during the second and third quarters of the sixteenth century plaques of pierced silver were used on backgrounds of brass-gilt and less frequently pierced gold plaques were laid on blued steel.

Piercing on its own was insufficient because the surface left after casting was rough. The case was therefore finished by chiselling or engraving.

Chiselling

Chiselling with a hammer and shaped punches was the original method of cleaning up pierced work after casting. The watchmaker thus removed unwanted metal, defined the design more and gave it an acceptable finish. By the middle of the sixteenth century work of this kind was being produced to perfection.

During the seventeenth century the art of chiselling was also applied to solid metal. There are some very beautiful gold and silver cases with pictures and designs worked in relief by this method.

Engraving

Engraving could be applied to pierced work and solid work alike.

An engraving tool cut a fine V groove in the metal and produced a more delicate result than was possible by chiselling. This technique was first used on watch cases about 1525 and by the end of the century it was common. Sometimes engraving and chiselling were used together. The bulk of the metal was removed by chiselling leaving the pattern in relief, and the pattern and chiselled work were finished with engraving.

Repoussé

In the art of repoussé soft sheet metal such as gold or silver was worked on from the back with hammer and punches, and the design or picture was produced in relief. The work was sometimes soldered to a brass-gilt plate. Repoussé is an ancient craft but it was not used on watch cases until the last quarter of the seventeenth century.

Niello

Niello was another form of decoration applied to cases. A design was worked in metal by chiselling or engraving, and the grooves were filled with a black composition. Originally watchmakers used an alloy of lead, copper and silver, mixed it in its molten state with sulphides and ran it into the work. Niello is rarely seen on watch cases dated before about 1620.

Guilloché (Engine Turning)

In guilloché work a turning-lathe was used to produce geometric patterns of intersecting and interlacing curved lines by fine shallow engraving. Such embellishment is frequently found on the backs of watch cases dated after about 1780. A layer of transparent or translucent enamel was frequently applied to give protection and added luster.

Enamel

Frequently, ornamentation was created by the application of enamel to metal, a form of art that was practiced in the East in ancient times. The enamel was made of glass or a vitreous composition consisting of silica, potash and red lead.

The melting point of these mixed powders varies with the proportion of the ingredients. A low melting temperature produces a soft enamel whereas a high melting temperature results in a hard enamel. Soft enamel scratches easily and its surface deteriorates after prolonged exposure. Hard enamel has little resistance to shock and is easily cracked and chipped, but in its favor is the ability to retain its color and glazed surface indefinitely.

The watchmaker raised the temperature of such a mixture to the point of fusing and introduced metal oxides to give color to what would otherwise have been a transparent flux. A vitreous coating was then applied to the metal and fused.

If a metal case were enamelled on one side only and then subjected to temperatures such as one might experience from the sun in tropic zones, the enamel would probably crack on account of distortion caused by the different rates of expansion of metal and enamel. To prevent this from happening the watchmaker always applied enamel to both sides of the metal which could then expand at the same rate without causing material stress.

At the end of the sixteenth century a few German watches were fitted with plain enamel dials; otherwise enamelling was not generally used until about 1630.

The principle methods of application were the following:

1. champlevé
2. cloisonné
3. painting in enamel
4. painting on enamel
5. basse-taille

Champlevé. Within the outlines of a pattern or design small cells were cut in the metal plate by a graver and then filled with powdered enamel, usually only one color to each cell. The cells were sometimes so close together that the dividing walls were almost too thin to be seen. The plate was fired and when the powder fused it shrank; so repeated applications of the powder and subsequent firings were required to bring the enamel slightly above the level of the metal plate. The enamel was then ground down to the level of the metal and polished, or given a quick firing to restore the glazed surface.

When translucent enamels were used the degree of color was influenced by the depth of the cells.

Cloisonné. This method of applying enamel differed from champlevé only in the way in which the cells were made. Thin narrow strips of gold were shaped to form the cells which were then placed edgeways on to an enamelled plate and fused.

To add brilliance to their colors, enamellers sometimes shaped pieces of silver or gold foil, known as paillons, and placed them at the bottom of each cell before applying translucent enamels to cloisonné and champlevé work.

Painting in enamel. This process started in Limoges, in about 1500, and during the middle years of the century some very beautiful floral work was produced. The technique was to deposit colored enamels to form a pattern on an enamelled plate and fire it without the aid of cells or cloisons to maintain separation. It was eminently suited to large flat areas but impossible on small curved surfaces such as watch cases.

Nevertheless, at the beginning of the seventeenth century a simplified form was applied to watch cases with great success. The case was first enamelled and then tiny globules of colored enamel were added before firing. The work was withdrawn from the heat as soon as the colors fused so that the design remained in relief. This technique was in general use during the first half of the century and many of the finest enamel watches come from this period.

Painting on enamel. About 1630 Jean Toutin, a French goldsmith working in Blois, developed a new technique in enamelling which made possible the reproduction of very fine detail in miniature.

The watch case was enamelled and the area to be painted was given a fine matt surface to assist the flow of the paint. Metal oxides provided the colors and these were mixed with small quantities of powdered flux to make them vitrifiable.

The colors were applied by brush, and pictures of human figures, landscapes, animals, floral arrangements and portraits were painted with remarkable accuracy and delicacy of touch.

When the brushwork was complete the artist fused the enamel by firing it. He then protected the picture by covering it with transparent flux and firing again.

Other artists followed Toutin's lead and soon Blois became the center of enamel painting; and it was from here that the most exquisitely designed and brilliantly colored enamel work was produced. Unfortunately the period of ultimate perfection was short-lived. By 1650 colors began losing much of their brilliance and there was a decline in the quality of pictures portraying the human figure. It became fashionable to paint voluptuous ladies in flimsy wraps displaying their charms to the eager gazes of old men.

Jean Toutin had two sons, Henri and Jean, both of whom studied under their father. Other great masters in Blois during the seventeenth century were Pierre Chartier, Isaac Gribelin, Dubie, Christopher Morlière, Robert Vanquer and Jacques Poëte. Chartier, Morlière and Poëte were particularly famous for their floral paintings. Knowledge of this new technique found its way to Switzerland and in 1635 Pierre Huaud began using it in Geneva.

In 1650, Jean Petitot, a student of Blois brushwork, founded a school for enamellers in Geneva and quickly established himself as a master of miniature portraiture for which work he was renowned in France and England.

Of Pierre Huaud's work none is known to have survived, but there exist a number of watches painted by his three sons, Pierre, Jean and Amy. Pierre was the first-born and the most skillful.

It is notable that until about 1675 it was very unusual for a painter on enamel to append a signature to his work. Fortunately for collectors, this omission was rectified by the Huaud brothers who always signed their work.

The earliest known work of Pierre dates to 1679. He worked in Geneva up to 1685 during which time he signed his work ''Huaut l'aisné.'' In 1685 he was appointed to the Court of Brandenburg and his various signatures were ''P. Huaud primogenitus,'' ''Pierre Huaud,'' and ''Petrus Huaud major natus.''

At first Jean worked on his own and signed himself ''Huaud le puisné,'' but it was not long before he and Amy worked together.

Up to 1686 the two brothers signed themselves ''Les deux frères Huaut les jeunes.'' They were then appointed to the Court of Prussia and worked in Berlin until 1700. During those years they signed themselves ''Les frères Huaud,'' sometimes adding the title ''peintres de son A. E. à Berlin.''

They returned to Geneva at the beginning of the eighteenth century and their paintings bore the signatures ''Les frères Huaud,'' ''Peter et Amicus Huaut,'' ''Fratres Huault,'' or ''Frères Huaut.''

Other painters who followed the example of the Huaud brothers by signing their work were Pierre Lignac, Jean Mussard, Jean André, Pierre Bordieu and Jean Louis Durand.

Although other countries adopted this new method of painting on enamel, the two main centers remained Blois and Geneva.

Until 1650 the French painters remained supreme but when the quality of their work declined it became little better than that of their foreign competitors. Slowly the lead was taken by painters in Geneva and towards the end of the eighteenth century their output was quite considerable; they had by that time established themselves as masters of the art. Nevertheless, for brilliance of color and for sheer beauty and delicacy of brushwork there have never been paintings to equal those of the Blois artists during the first half of the seventeenth century.

Basse-Taille. This was a most distinctive form of decoration in which a film of colored transparent enamel was applied to a metal case, usually gold, which had an engraved symmetrical design. It became very popular at the end of the eighteenth century when it was applied to guilloché work.

Shagreen

Shagreen, the skin of a shark or ray fish, was frequently used as a protective outer case for watches. It was first dried and then ground flat and polished. Because of shagreen's granular structure the result was a finished surface covered by irregularly shaped rings.

Sometimes craftsmen used a leather imitation, produced from the skin of horses, donkeys or camels, and introduced the granular effect by pressing hard round seeds into the skin while it was wet, then maintaining the pressure until the skin dried out. Next it was ground, polished and dyed green to resemble genuine shagreen. The leather was then secured to the metal case of the watch by pinwork.

Filigree

Filigree, ornamental lacework of gold and silver wire was another means of embellishment. The wire was twisted into shapes which were laid one on top of the other and held by solder.

Piqué

The application of gold and silver pins to outer cases is called piqué. Early pair-cases were separate from watches and were shaped from stiff leather. Gold and silver pins or studs were used to produce an endless variety of designs.

When the outer case became part of the watch, about 1650, it was made of shell or metal. Shell cases were frequently decorated with piqué. Metal cases were covered with leather or shagreen to which piqué was also applied. In such instances the pins, in addition to being decorative, helped considerably in holding the skin covering to the metal case.

Another application of piqué was in the form of inlaid work on tortoise-shell. The shell was cut with narrow grooves and heated. Thin strips of gold or silver were then inserted into the grooves under pressure.

CHAPTER 9
Some Famous Makers

The Worshipful Company of Clockmakers

During the sixteenth century French blacksmiths who had learned the art of clockmaking journeyed to London to make iron chamber clocks. Their skills were copied by English blacksmiths and by the end of the century clockmaking in England had become established.

In 1578 the Blacksmiths Company was incorporated in England to look after the interests of blacksmiths. When many of its members turned their hands to the manufacture of clocks the Blacksmiths Company extended its interests to include the new trade.

In 1627 French clockmakers asked that letters patent be granted so that they could continue their clockmaking in London on a more permanent basis. Such license would have resulted in English clockmakers being faced with serious competition and they felt that the Blacksmiths Company was insufficiently influential to safeguard their interests and that the time had come to form their own guild.

In 1630 a group of prominent London clockmakers and some Freemen of the Blacksmiths Company formed a committee and petitioned Charles I for a charter. The request was granted and in 1631 a Royal Charter was issued and The Worshipful Company of Clockmakers was formed in London, the men responsible being enrolled as Brothers. They had no building of their own and meetings were conducted in taverns.

The functions of the Company were to safeguard the interests of its members and those of the public, and to ensure adequate training of apprentices under proper supervision and without exploitation.

The Company had authority over clockmakers within a radius of ten miles of the City of London. It had power to introduce its own by-laws and the authority to ensure that they were carried out, by force if necessary. General control was also exercised over all clockmakers throughout the kingdom.

The first task of the Company was to secure the position of English clockmakers. It was made illegal for any foreigner to work in London as a clockmaker unless he was employed by a member of the Company. A law was introduced forbidding the importation of clocks and watches, and the Company had authority to inspect the cargoes of ships and the contents of warehouses. Any resistance to entry was met by force with police in attendance.

Improved working conditions were introduced and employers were required to conform to the new standards.

In the interest of the public, efforts were made to eliminate the possibility of inferior work being produced. The Company had authority to visit workshops and destory any faulty or shoddy work, and power to impose fines on clockmakers contravening any of the Company by-laws. This right of search continued into the reign of William III until it was abolished in 1700.

New regulations were introduced governing the administration and training of apprentices. No clockmaker was allowed to employ an apprentice unless he, himself, was a member of The Worshipful Company of Clockmakers. The period of training had to be seven years, at the successful conclusion of which the trainee was admitted as a Freeman clockmaker. A further period of two years was then required to be spent in the workshop of his master or any other master as a journeyman, after which he was called upon by the Company to make a piece of work of their choosing which was referred to as a masterpiece. When the work was complete it was submitted to the Master and Wardens of the Company and if approved, the Freeman was registered as a Master clockmaker. It was from the ranks of the Master clockmakers that England produced their most eminent clock and watchmakers.

Arnold, John (1736-1799)

John Arnold was born at Bodmin in Cornwall, England, and served an apprenticeship as a watchmaker with his father. About 1760 he moved to premises in Fleet Street, London, and it was not long before he established himself as an horologist of considerable skill and delicacy of touch. He made a half quarter repeating watch so small that the movement was scarcely more than nine millimeters in diameter. He used a cylinder escapement and made the cylinder of ruby; it was the first of its kind. The watch was set in a ring and in 1764 he presented it to George III. The king was so impressed with the fineness of the work that he acknowledged the gift with five hundred guinea pieces.

During that year Harrison's No. 4 sailed to Barbados on board the ''Tartar'' and underwent its second successful trial. This achievement made a deep impression on Arnold and he began taking an active interest in the calculation of longitude at sea.

By 1770 he had made his first pocket chronometer and fitted a pivoted detent escapement of his own design. His first attempts were failures but he persevered, and it was not long before he produced a pivoted detent that gave a good account of itself.

He had made several chronometers by 1773 and was experimenting with bimetallic compensators. His idea was to apply temperature compensation to the balance instead of to the balance spring as in the case of Harrison's compensation curb.

In 1776 he found that helical springs produced results better than those achieved by flat spiral springs, and then, in 1782, he discovered that if the ends of helical springs were turned inward, isochronism was introduced.

Arnold had introduced a spring detent in 1780 and his application for a patent had been unsuccessfully challenged by Thomas Earnshaw.

After ten years of experimenting with bimetallic compensators, Arnold produced, in 1783, the first bimetallic cut balance.

Altogether, John Arnold made over nine hundred chronometers and it was his proud claim that no two movements were the same. He used an irregular system of fractional numbering that unfortunately is of little help in dating his work. The fractional numbers used for chronometers were consistent in that the numerator and denominator always differed by ninety. This does not apply to his watches.

Arnold was admitted as a member of the Company of Clockmakers in 1783.

Arnold, John Roger

John Roger Arnold was the son of John Arnold. His father arranged for him to serve an apprenticeship with Abraham-Louis Breguet, the celebrated French watchmaker, in Paris. Then, in 1787, he entered into partnership with his father, after which all Arnold instruments carried the signature "John Arnold and Son," instead of the earlier signature "John Arnold."

After his father's death John Roger carried on the business in his own name. Both he and his foreman, Thomas Prest, were capable of producing instruments of very high quality and the firm continued making excellent pocket chronometers.

Whether or not Prest remained in the employ of John Roger is uncertain, but we do know that in 1830 John Roger entered into a ten year partnership with E. J. Dent. During that time the business thrived although John Roger became progressively more inactive in his business affairs. At the end of the ten year agreement, Dent opted out and set up in business on his own account taking with him much of the firm's goodwill and customers.

John Roger died three years later in 1843. His exact age is not known, but if we assume he was twenty-one years at the time he joined his father in business he would have been seventy-seven years at the time of his death.

He was made a member of the Company of Clockmakers in 1796 and a master in 1817.

Barlow, Edward (1636-1716)

Edward Barlow adopted the name of his godfather, his original name being Booth. He devoted much of his time to the study of horological instruments and in 1676 invented the rack striking mechanism for clocks. The same year he most ably demonstrated how his invention made possible the introduction of a repeat mechanism.

In 1686 he made a repeater watch and applied for a patent, but Daniel Quare who had been making repeater watches since 1680 successfully opposed Barlow's application.

Berthoud, Ferdinand (1727-1807)

There were a number of makers bearing the name Berthoud, most of whom were related. The most famous was Ferdinand. He was born in Neuchâtel, Switzerland. At an early age he showed a pronounced aptitude for understanding technical subjects and at the age of fourteen was allowed to commence training as a watchmaker. His ability to absorb information was only a little short of being uncanny. He studied the work of eminent makers of his time and wrote interesting and constructive papers.

While a young man he earned for himself a reputation of being an exceptional maker of fine instruments and in 1762 was appointed Horloger de la Marine. He afterwards became absorbed in extensive research into the design of marine timekeepers and made over seventy such instruments. Some of his work can be seen at the Musée des Arts et Métiers, Paris.

Berthoud also made some very fine clocks and regulators and produced his own detent escapement for use with pendulum clocks.

In his lifetime he committed to paper a wealth of horological information and for this work many seats of learning conferred distinctions upon him.

Breguet, Abraham-Louis (1747-1823)

Abraham-Louis Breguet is the man who is sometimes described as the greatest horologist of all time. This may be elevating his status a little more than is justified, but there is no doubt that he was the most famous watchmaker during his lifetime.

He was born in Neuchâtel, Switzerland, and when he was fifteen he entered into an apprenticeship with a watchmaker in Versailles, France. When his training was complete it is thought that he worked for Berthoud, and it seems evident that in 1782 he started working for himself.

Documentary evidence of his business activities is recorded in the now famous Breguet books but they were not started until 1787.

When the guillotine was set up in 1793, during the early days of the French Revolution, Breguet fled the country in fear for his life. He lived first in Switzerland and later journeyed to England where he stayed until the Revolution was over. In 1795 he returned to Paris and rebuilt his business.

Breguet made clocks, chronometers and watches, but he is most famous for his watches. He introduced a style that set the pattern for the modern watch. He had a tremendous capacity for horological invention and was always willing to make a watch to suit a customer's particular requirement. A perfectionist and an artist, Breguet's taste was beyond criticism. Altogether, he made about four thousand watches and, apart from his montres à souscription, no two were ever identical.

Bréguet died at the age of seventy-six having earned a worldwide reputation. His influence lived on and, indeed, many features of modern watches can be traced back directly to his workshop in Paris.

Brockbank, John and Myles

For a little under a century the Brockbank family operated from premises at 6 Cowper's Court, Cornhill, London, as watch and chronometer makers. The most famous were John and his younger brother Myles.

In 1771 John Brockbank became a customer of Thomas Earnshaw in that he paid Earnshaw to do work for him. In 1780 Earnshaw invented a spring detent and showed it to John Brockbank who considered the design well worth covering by a patent and advised Earnshaw accordingly. Lack of funds prevented Earnshaw from taking this action and three years later, when Arnold produced his own spring detent, Earnshaw accused the Brockbanks of betraying a confidence.

Peto was an employee of the Brockbank brothers. He designed his own form of spring detent which was a combination of the spring detents introduced by Earnshaw and Arnold. It became known as the cross-detent escapement and examples of Brockbank instruments fitted with Peto's escapement still exist.

The two brothers consistently produced very high class work throughout their business career. John died early in the nineteenth century and Myles retired in 1808. The business was taken over by their nephews, also named John and Myles, who continued trading as John Brockbank & Co. until 1812. The company name was then changed to Brockbank & Grove until 1814, Brockbank & Atkins until 1835, and Brockbank, Atkins & Son until 1842.

Debaufre, Peter (1689-1722)

Peter Debaufre came from a French family of distinguished horologists. He went to London from Paris and started his own watchmaking business in Soho. In 1689 he was admitted to the Company of Clockmakers.

Also living in London was a Swiss, Nicholas Facio de Duillier who, with the help of Peter and his brother Jacob, discovered a method of cutting and piercing stones for use as pivot holes. A patent was granted to Facio in 1704.

Peter Debaufre invented an escapement having two escape wheels mounted parallel with each other and separated by a common pallet. The wheels were so positioned that the impulse face of the pallet was acted on by teeth of both wheels alternately. Such a watch was owned by Sir Isaac Newton who spoke highly of its performance.

Even so, the movement was not popular and remained in isolation until revived by Peter Litherland of Liverpool at the end of the century.

Earnshaw, Thomas (1749-1829)

Thomas Earnshaw was born at Ashton-under-Lyne, England. At the age of fourteen he entered into an apprenticeship with a watchmaker. When his training was finished he journeyed to London where he started a business as a watch movement finisher.

In 1780 Earnshaw designed a spring detent for use with chronometer escapements claiming that such an arrangement produced superior results over those obtained from a pivoted detent. He explained his idea to John Brockbank whose opinions he valued. Brockbank strongly advised Earnshaw to protect his idea with a patent. Unfortunately, Earnshaw was not able to pay for a patent and for this reason he approached a customer, Thomas Wright.

It was agreed that if Earnshaw made an instrument fitted with the new spring detent then Wright would apply for a patent. Unfortunately, Wright delayed in submitting the application until 1783 when it was discovered that Arnold had already introduced the idea. Earnshaw was furious with Wright and accused him of dilatory behavior. The Brockbank brothers were next in line for Earnshaw's anger; they were accused of divulging to Arnold details of Earnshaw's invention but there was no evidence to support this.

When compared with Arnold's large and highly finished marine chronometers, Earnshaw's instruments were very small and dull in appearance. Earnshaw made them this way to keep down the cost, but not at the expense of accuracy and reliability. Very few of Earnshaw's marine chronometers have survived but fortunately his pocket chronometers are not so scarce.

It was Earnshaw who introduced fusing together the two metals of a bimetallic balance. Whereas the brass and steel strips were soldered or riveted together, Earnshaw poured molten brass over a steel disc and lathe turned the result to produce a bimetallic wheel.

In 1794 he succeeded to the business of William Hughes in High Holborn, London, and when he died the business was carried on by his son Thomas.

Ellicott, John (1706-1772)

John Ellicott was born in London and was the most distinguished watch and clockmaker in the Ellicott family. His father, also John, was an excellent watchmaker and was admitted to the Company of Clockmakers in 1696.

In 1728 the younger Ellicott started a business in Sweeting's Alley near the Royal Exchange. In 1838 the old Royal Exchange was destoryed by fire and Sweeting's Alley was never rebuilt.

Ellicott watches are serial numbered and number 123 dates about the time John Ellicott set up in Sweeting's Alley. He was a maker of fine watches and clocks and designed several of London's public clocks.

In 1738 he became a Fellow of the Royal Society and was later appointed clockmaker to George II. When he died his business was continued by his son Edward who had been in partnership with him from 1760.

Edward died in 1791 and the business passed to his son, also an Edward, who, in 1834, was elected master of the Company of Clockmakers. He died the following year.

Prior to about 1750 watches were signed "Jno Ellicott"; early watches were frequently signed beneath the cock or balance. The signature then changed to "Ellicott" or "John Ellicott and Son."

About 1791 the signature became "Edward Ellicott and Sons," and was later changed to "Ellicott & Taylor" when the second Edward took on a partner from about 1811 to 1830. From then until 1840 watches were signed "Ellicott & Smith."

The following table of serial numbers is a guide to the date of an Ellicott watch.

Serial Number	Year
123	1728
400	1730
1800	1740
3250	1750
4770	1760
6435	1770
7620	1780
8450	1790
8760	1800
9074	1810

Emery, Josiah (1725-1797)

Josiah Emery was born in Switzerland but settled in England. He started a clock and watchmaking business at 33 Cockspur Street, London, where he made exceptionally fine cylinder watches. He also made a number of pocket watches fitted with pivoted detent escapements.

For his work in developing the lever escapement Josiah Emery is most famed. The escapement was invented by Thomas Mudge in 1754 who made only one lever watch. This he presented to George III in 1770. At the age of sixty-seven Mudge made a rough model of his escapement which was handed to Emery for him to copy. After completing this work Emery went on to develop the idea. In all he made about thirty-five lever watches between 1782 and 1795 of which only twelve are known to have survived.

After Emery's death the business was carried on by Louis Recordon.

Facio, Nicholas (1664-1753)

Nicholas Facio was born in Basle and in 1687 he settled in England. It was he, in association with the Debaufre brothers, who devised the means of cutting and drilling precious stones to be used as bearings for arbor pivots. An application for a patent was granted but the Company of Clockmakers defeated a subsequent application to extend the period in the interests of lapidaries (gem-cutters). However, the English kept the secret for almost a century during which time they enjoyed a monopoly.

Graham, George (1673-1751)

George Graham was born among England's lakes in the county of Cumberland. At an early age he tramped his way to London, a distance of nearly three hundred miles, where, in 1688, he became apprenticed to Henry Aske until 1695.

At the completion of his apprenticeship he was admitted as a freeman of the Company of Clockmakers and went to work for Thomas Tompion. The following year he married Tompion's niece Elizabeth.

A deep and lasting friendship developed between master and pupil and, with Tompion's tuition, Graham's skill and knowledge came at least to equal that of Tompion himself. During the latter part of

Tompion's life Graham managed his old master's affairs and during these last few years some clocks were engraved with both their names on the dial.

In 1713 Tompion died at the age of seventy-four leaving his business to his friend Graham who remained for the next seven years at the Dial and Three Crowns in Fleet Street. He became known as "honest George Graham" and was well liked and respected for his kindness and generosity.

Graham invented the dead beat escapement for clocks in 1715. This was a very valued contribution towards achieving precise timekeeping.

Premises across the road from the Dial and Three Crowns became vacant in 1720 and Graham moved his business naming the new establishment Dial and One Crown. He became well known for his papers on horological matters and was highly respected for his skill in making mathematical instruments for astronomical studies and observation. He was involved in the design of England's first planetarium. For his work in this field he was made a Fellow of the Royal Society in 1721, and the following year was elected master of the Company of Clockmakers.

In 1726 Graham invented the mercury compensated pendulum, and this, used in combination with his dead beat escapement, produced an accuracy in clock timekeeping never before attained.

Graham continued Tompion's practice of numbering clocks. He commenced at 600 and finished at 774, a total of one hundred and seventy-four timepieces.

During 1725 and 1726 Graham further developed the cylinder escapement for watches and brought its performance to a high standard which has been little improved since. After 1726 he fitted the cylinder escapement to all his watches.

In 1728 Julien Le Roy journeyed from France to England to visit Graham and was shown the cylinder escapement. Le Roy was so impressed with it that on his return to France he adopted it for use in his own watches.

Prior to about 1726 Graham's watches were fitted with verge escapements and the earliest of these had balance cocks with pierced feet. He then changed the style and subsequent watches were fitted with cocks that had solid feet decorated with engraving. A large diamond endstone was provided for the balance staff pivot.

Hands were usually beetle and poker style fashioned from blued steel. Some watches were fitted with steel center seconds hands, delicately shaped and polished. These watches were usually fitted with stop work but their disadvantage was that the time train stopped when the mechanism was operated.

Graham made nearly six hundred repeaters but, despite the additional mechanism on this type of watch, they were almost invariably smaller than his plain watches.

Altogether, Graham made about three thousand watches. He employed two series of numbers, one for his plain watches and the other for repeaters. As a guide, the following numbers are listed showing their hallmark dates.

Repeaters		Plain Watches	
Number	Year	Number	Year
393	1713	4669	1715
480	1720	5260	1725
620	1730	5610	1735
790	1740	6180	1745
883	1745	6480	1750
960	1750	6574	1751
965	1751		

Graham engraved the number, along with his signature, on the top plate and stamped the number on the bottom plate beneath the dial and underneath the balance cock. This is usually an indication of whether the watch is a genuine Graham or one of the many fakes that came from Europe.

Such was the esteem held by the English for both Tompion and Graham that they were buried in Westminster Abbey in the same grave.

Harrison, John (1693-1776)

John Harrison was born at Foulby in Yorkshire, England, and when he was seven his parents moved to Barrow in Lincolnshire. Harrison had been brought up to be a carpenter like his father, but he had an aptitude for mechanical things and it was not long before he was taking an interest in clocks.

Harrison's ability as a clockmaker was the result of being self-taught, and because he had not served an apprenticeship he was not eligible for acceptance into the Company of Clockmakers. His earliest efforts in the field of horology were to clean and repair clocks. He then went on to make grandfather clock cases. In 1715 he completed two grandfather clocks, each with movements almost entirely of wood that produced remarkably accurate timekeeping. One of these clocks can be seen in the Science Museum, London. It is wound by a key, the holes for which are in the bottom corners of the dial and hidden by removable spandrel ornaments.

About 1726 Harrison produced three inventions. The first was the gridiron compensating pendulum that was designed to take advantage of the differing rates of expansion of steel and brass rods. The second was the grasshopper escapement. This was an arrangement similar in action to an anchor escapement except that the pallets were pivoted to the anchor and held in place by light spring pressure. The pallets were frequently made of lignum vitae. The third invention was another form of maintaining power, sometimes called Harrison's maintaining spring. When the pull of the weight turned a barrel, a spring was compressed against the main wheel causing the main wheel to rotate. When the barrel was turned in the reverse direction during winding, the spring pressure was retained by a ratchet and was sufficient to keep the time train going until winding was complete. This principle of maintaining power is in general use today in regulators and fusee chronometers.

By far the greatest of Harrison's achievements was his production of five marine timekeepers, a task to which he devoted more than half his life (see Chapter Five).

Houriet, Jacques Frédéric (1743-1830)

Jacques Frédéric Houriet was an outstanding Swiss watchmaker who at one time worked for Breguet. He is particularly noted for his exceptionally fine tourbillons and chronometers. In 1814 he introduced the spherical balance spring.

Jürgensen, Urban (1776-1830)

Urban Jürgensen was born in Copenhagen, the son of a Danish watchmaker. The early years of his training were spent in his father's workshop.

In 1796 he commenced a further period of training under Jacques Houriet and then, in 1800, he went to Paris where he studied with Breguet and Berthoud. In 1801 he went to London and completed his studies with Arnold.

Jürgensen returned to Copenhagen and started his own business making chronometers and watches. Many of the chronometers were for the Danish navy. The quality of his work was always of the highest. Altogether he made nearly nine hundred instruments the majority of which were in silver cases.

After his death he was succeeded by his sons, Louis Urban (1806-1867) and Jules Frederick (1808-1877).

Le Roy, Julien (1686-1759)

Julien Le Roy was the son of a clockmaker who lived in Tours, France. In 1699 Julien entered into an apprenticeship with Alex. Le Bon, a Parisian maker of fine equation clocks.

In 1725 he invented the adjustable potence for verge watches. This was an arrangement that allowed the lateral position of the crown escape wheel to be adjusted in relation to the verge. In addition, he provided an adjusting screw to alter the depthing of the crown wheel teeth with the verge pallets. Prior to this invention it had been necessary to disassemble the movement to adjust the escapement.

In 1727, when visiting George Graham in London, Le Roy was given a cylinder watch, and he was so favorably impressed that on his return to France he fitted cylinder escapements to all his subsequent watches.

His work was so excellent, and his influence among French makers so outstanding, that in 1739 he was appointed clockmaker to Louis XV with living accommodations at the Louvre.

Le Roy is particularly famous for his very fine repeaters. He invented a miniature form of anchor escapement designed to regulate the speed of striking. About the middle of the eighteenth century he dispensed with the use of bells and replaced them with wire gongs. This greatly assisted in the subsequent development of slim watches. Le Roy was also the first to make dumb repeaters. He arranged for a metal block to receive the hammer blows instead of using wire gongs; in this way the wearer would feel the strikes but hear little or no sound.

With the help of his lifelong friend, Henry Sully, the English inventor of oil sinks, Le Roy lifted the status of French clock and watch making to a new high level. This fine craftsmanship was to be continued by his son Pierre and later by Breguet, finally winning back for France the supremacy that the English had held for so long.

Le Roy, Pierre (1717-1785)

Pierre Le Roy was the eldest son of Julien and he succeeded his father in business. At an early age he developed an interest in the making of marine timekeepers to which he devoted most of his working life.

In 1748 Le Roy invented a new form of escapement which enabled the balance to swing almost free of any mechanical interference. He called it his detent escapement.

In 1750 he invented another form of escapement which was called the duplex. It was never popular in France but during the first half of the nineteenth century it was revived and widely used in England.

At the death of his father in 1759, Le Roy was granted the honor of appointment to Louis XV.

In 1766 he completed his final work on marine timekeepers. It was a masterpiece of design and workmanship and included the three essentials of a precise timepiece, i.e. a detached escapement, a compensated balance and an isochronous balance spring. It was tested at sea, and it seems that its performance was equal to that of Harrison's No. 4 which had undergone its first sea trial only five years earlier.

Poor health decided Pierre to retire, and, undoubtedly discouraged at receiving no official recognition for his work, he took up residence in the country where he spent his remaining years.

Mudge, Thomas (1715-1794)

Thomas Mudge was born at Exeter in the county of Devon, England. His father was a clergyman. At an early age Mudge showed a distinct interest in mechanics and when he was sixteen his father apprenticed him to George Graham in London.

Mudge showed great promise and under Graham's tuition he quickly developed into a watch and clockmaker of unusual talent. On the completion of his training he was given a position of some responsibility in Graham's business at the sign of the Dial and One Crown on Fleet Street. In 1738 he was admitted to the Company of Clockmakers.

Mudge remained in Graham's employ until his master died in 1751 and then went into business on his own.

His mastery of the art of watchmaking had long been established and he was asked by Ferdinand VI of Spain to make a timekeeper of unique design. This he did in the form of a striking watch with repeat mechanism and equation work set in the head of a walking cane.

In 1755 Mudge entered into partnership with William Dutton who also had been apprenticed to Graham. Together, these two men produced watches of great elegance and accuracy.

In 1759 Mudge made horological history when he made a pocket watch for George III. It was the first watch that automatically compensated for changes in temperature and also the first to be fitted with Mudge's invention of the lever escapement. The watch is now in Windsor Castle in the care of the royal family and is still in going order.

Mudge had been making a study of the requirements of marine timekeepers and in 1765 he wrote a paper on the subject.

In 1771 he left the running of the Fleet Street business to William Dutton and took up residence in Plymouth where he was able to pursue his nautical studies. Three years later he made his first marine chronometer and sent it to Greenwich Observatory for trial. Admiral Campbell took the timepiece on a voyage to Newfoundland and, on his arrival back in England, reported that the chronometer readings had been satisfactory. As a result of this, the Board of Longitude paid Mudge the sum of £500 requesting he continue with his research.

In the meantime, in 1776, Mudge received the honor of being appointed clockmaker to George III.

In 1779 Mudge sent two more marine chronometers to Greenwich Observatory for trial. After years of indecision the British Government finally decided in 1793 to pay Mudge a further £2,500 for his work, but it was too late for him to enjoy. He died a few months later.

Quare, Daniel. (1647-1724)

Daniel Quare was born in the county of Somerset, England, and brought up as a Quaker. He served an apprenticeship with a clockmaker and then went to London where, in 1671, he was admitted to the Company of Clockmakers. The same year he started a clockmaking business at St. Martins le Grand, London, and while at these premises he married into a wealthy and influential Quaker family.

The business was a success and Quare produced some very fine clocks. In 1680 he invented a repeater mechanism that he used in clocks and watches.

About this time he vacated St. Martins le Grand to take up residence in Exchange Alley, London, under the sign of The Kings Arms.

In 1686 Edward Barlow invented a form of repeater mechanism and applied for a patent to safeguard his interests. However, the Company of Clockmakers submitted Barlow's application to the Privy Council, recommending that a patent not be granted since Quare had been producing clocks and watches with a similar mechanism for some years.

It was the opinion of King James II that Quare and Barlow should each submit a watch fitted with his own repeater mechanism. This they did. Quare's watch had a short pin projecting from the edge of the case near the pendant which, when depressed, sounded the hour and the quarter. Barlow's watch had two pins, one for the hour and the other for the quarter. The king showed a preference for Quare's watch.

Quare specialized in making grandfather clocks of long duration, many of which ran twelve months between winds. He also made equation clocks.

Near the end of the seventeenth century he experimented with barometric instruments and in 1695 he was granted a patent for a portable barometer.

In 1708 Quare was elected master of the Company of Clockmakers. Shortly after George I took the throne Quare was appointed clockmaker to the king, but he refused to take the Oath of Allegiance that was required by all persons entering the royal palace. The problem was overcome when permission was given to allow Quare to use the servants' entrance at the rear.

In later years Quare took a partner, Stephen Horseman, who had been in Quare's employ since the beginning of his apprenticeship in 1701. The business continued to flourish under the new name of Quare and Horseman.

Tompion, Thomas (1639-1713)

Thomas Tompion was England's most famous clockmaker and is frequently referred to as the father of English clockmakers. He was born at Ickwell Green near the village of Northill in the county of Bedfordshire. Tompion's father and grandfather had both been village blacksmiths in their time and Tompion grew up in the environment of a forge. The blacksmith's workshop still exists. It has become a building of historic interest and proudly displays a plaque in commemoration of Tompion.

Records are vague as to how Tompion spent his early life. It is known that he journeyed to London where a clockmaker must have been befriended and apprenticed him because in 1671 he was accepted into the Company of Clockmakers.

In 1674 Tompion took over premises at the corner of Fleet Street and Water Lane (now Whitefriars Street) where he started a business under the sign of the Dial and Three Crowns. He remained a bachelor but as time passed his household grew. He provided accommodation for relations, journeymen, apprentices and servants. The premises were partly used for workshops and at the front was a shop where he sold clocks and watches Among his relations was a niece who married Edward Banger a clockmaker employed by Tompion.

Shortly after moving into the house in Water Lane Tompion met Dr. Robert Hooke and a friendship developed. Hooke was a scientist and mathematician and produced a never ending supply of new ideas, but he needed a man with creative skill to put his ideas into practice. Hooke was a man with influence and some of Tompion's work came to the attention of Charles II and the Astronomer Royal.

Hooke invented a form of spiral balance spring for use in pocket watches, and Tompion included Hooke's design in a watch which he presented to Charles II. It should be noted that Christiaan Huygens had also invented a spiral balance spring and watches were being made in Paris incorporating this new idea.

In 1676 Tompion was asked to make the first clocks ever to be installed in Greenwich Observatory. He made two timepieces each with a duration of one year. In the same year he introduced rack striking, an invention of Edward Barlow, and included this new mechanism in all his later clocks.

In 1695 Tompion designed the first equation clock. The additional mechanism necessitated increasing the height of the dial which he did by extending it in semi-circular fashion. This new dial became known as the break-arch or broken-arch dial. The clock was presented to William III and was later handed down through the royal family and kept in Buckingham Palace where it is today.

The same year he engaged a new assistant, George Graham, fresh from apprenticeship. Graham was destined for great things and he became a lifelong friend of Tompion.

In 1701 Tompion and Edward Banger formed a partnership but it lasted scarcely more than six years breaking up in 1707.

Tompion's business grew and he became a man of wealth. How many clockmakers he employed is unknown, but it has been established that in his workshops he arranged for each man to become a specialist in making certain components, a practice that resulted in standardization and interchangeability of parts.

During his lifetime Tompion was famous for his watches but after his death he became better known for his clocks. Records indicate that he must have made about fifty-five hundred watches and something like six hundred and fifty clocks. About 1682 he started a system of numbering and it is known that clock numbers go up to five hundred and forty-two, but unfortunately they give no indication of the year of manufacture.

The dating of watches is a little less difficult and the following chart is a rough guide to the year of manufacture.

Watch Numbers

Repeaters	Other Watches	Signature	Year
203	3292	Thos Tompion	1701
196-290	3252-4119	Thos Tompion Edwd Banger	1701-1708
350-392	4265-4312	Thos Tompion	1708-1713
	4369-4543	T. Tompion & G. Graham	1711-1713

Hallmarking stamps are helpful but only with gold cases after about 1678. Silver cases were not hallmarked during Tompion's lifetime.

During Tompion's lifetime, and for many years after, unscrupulous makers forged his signature on their own watches. One indication of whether or not a watch is a fake is the location of the serial number; Tompion always stamped his watch numbers beneath the balance cock.

Tompion took little active part in the administration and functions of the Company of Clockmakers, being more inclined to go his own way within the limits of the Company regulations. Nevertheless, in 1703 he was elected master.

By this time Tompion had become the unchallenged leader among England's clockmakers and he was held in high esteem. In the world of horology he was a man of outstanding ability and some influence. Today he is famous the world over for his grandfather clocks and bracket clocks. Among his most ambitious pieces of work was a spring-driven quarter-striking ebonized bracket clock of one year's duration that was made for William III.

In recognition of his lifelong work the English honored Tompion by having him buried in Westminster Abbey.

CHAPTER 10
Glossary of Terms

Adjusted - A watch is said to be ''adjusted'' after any positional errors have been corrected and any variation in rate, due to temperature changes, have been compensated. The rating of a watch is checked in five positions, i.e. three vertical positions with dial markings 3, 9 and 12 uppermost, and two horizontal positions with dial up and dial down. These checks are conducted in two temperatures, about 42°F and 92°F. Such adjustments are not usually carried out on low-grade watches.

Affix - A small supplementary bimetallic strip attached at one end to a balance to compensate for the error of the balance during temperature changes. Affixes are fitted two to a balance and positioned diametrically opposite each other.

All-or-Nothing Piece - A piece added to the repeat mechanism to hold the repeating train until the release is fully depressed. With this modified mechanism fitted a repeater strikes all or nothing. The piece corrected a problem with early repeating watches, namely, that if the push piece or actuating lever was not fully pressed home insufficient strikes were made.

Amplitude - The maximum angle through which a balance swings right or left of its position of rest.

Anti-Magnetic - A term describing watches whose parts are made of non-magnetic material. The problem with early watches was that if the balance, balance spring or escapement operated within the influence of a magnetic field, or if any of these parts had been in contact with a permanent magnet, the rate of the watch was impaired. The first non-magnetic balance springs used were those fitted by John Arnold to his marine chronometers.

Appliqué - Detached ornaments, chapters and numerals that are applied to a dial, and various forms of decoration that are applied to cases.

Arbor - The spindle that holds a wheel or pinion, or both, of a watch. Even if a pinion and arbor are turned from one piece they are referred to by their separate names. In modern watches the arbors of balances and pallets are more commonly known as staffs.

Arc - The full angle of swing of a balance, or twice the amplitude. If the amplitude is 225° then the arc is 450° which means the balance swings through one and one quarter revolutions.

Assay - To determine the amount of gold or silver in a metal.

Automata - Animated figures of objects which are displayed on the dial and are activated by time or strike trains.

Automatic Winding - See Perpetual Watch.

Auxiliary Compensation - A device sometimes fitted to a bimetallic balance to overcome Middle Temperature Error.

Balance - A controller in the form of a wheel whose swinging motion governs one end of a train of wheels powered at the other end by a spring; the train then drives a set of hands. This arrangement of parts fulfills the basic requirements of a timekeeper. The description "balance wheel" is frequently heard but it is not an accepted horological term. Some of the earliest watches had plain balances fitted with two, three, and sometimes four, arms radiating from the center. It was not until 1675 that balance springs were added. See also Compensation Balance.

Balance Spring - A flat spiral balance spring is a light spring attached at its inner end to the balance staff, and at its outer end to the movement plate or balance cock. Such a spring is not Isochronous. Marine chronometers, and some high-grade pocket watches, use helical springs, i.e. a spring that is formed by being wound on a rod or tube.

Dr. Robert Hooke was the first to think seriously about using a balance spring, but it was Christiaan Huygens who, in 1675, first applied a flat spiral spring to the balance of a watch. It was found that a sprung balance was capable of regulating timekeeping far better than an uncontrolled balance without a spring.

Balance Staff - The arbor upon which the Balance is mounted.

Banking Pin - A device used to keep the swing of a balance within its designed limits. The balance of a verge escapement carries a pin that protrudes from its outer edge and makes contact with the balance cock if the balance overswings. With a lever escapement, two pins are positioned vertically in the movement plate, one on either side of the lever, and at a distance from each other to permit the lever freedom during its normal angular movement.

Baroque - A rough pearl.

Barred Movement - See Lepine Caliber.

Barrel - The cylindrical container in which the mainspring is coiled. When used with a fusee the barrel is plain. When used without a fusee it has teeth cut on the outside to form the great wheel; it is then known as a Going Barrel.

Barrel (Going) - A spring barrel used in a movement where no fusee is fitted. Teeth are cut around the outside of the barrel to form the great wheel. The mainspring is coiled inside the barrel. Its outer end is hooked to the inside wall and the inner end is anchored to the arbor in the center. Rotating the arbor with a key winds the spring until it is tightly coiled.

When the spring unwinds, the arbor is held stationary by a ratchet and click, and so the outer end of the spring has to move taking the barrel with it. The teeth of the great wheel thus drive the train.

Bascule - In a chronometer escapement, a detent that is designed to pivot. To avoid the need for lubrication, the detent is usually mounted on a spring instead.

Beat - The sound produced by the escape wheel teeth striking the pallets of the escapement.

Beetle Hand - A typical eighteenth century English hour hand that derives its name from the stag beetle whose shape it is supposed to resemble. It is used with a Poker minute hand.

Bezel - The metal rim that holds the glass.

Bimetallic - The result of riveting or fusing together two dissimilar metals. In watchmaking the metals used are brass and steel. The coefficients of expansion of these two metals are different and for any given rise in temperature the brass will expand more than the steel. If a bimetallic strip is secured at one end and then subjected to a temperature increase, the different coefficients of expansion will cause the strip to bend, the brass being on the outer face of the curve, and the free end will move. This is the principle upon which a Compensation Curb and a Compensation Balance function.

John Harrison was the first to use a bimetallic strip when he built his No. 3 marine timekeeper. See Chapter Five.

Bottom Plate - The plate nearest the dial. It is sometimes called the pillar plate because it is to the bottom plate that movement pillars are fixed.

Bow - The stirrup or ring that is looped or pivoted to the pendant to which a chain or fob is attached.

Breguet Hand - A style of watch hand that was very popular with Breguet. It has a narrow tapered shaft with an eccentrically pierced ring near the end looking rather like a full moon. Extending beyond the ring is a short slender arrow head. This type of hand is sometimes called a moon hand.

Breguet Key - A device whose shaft is made in two pieces which are joined by a spring-loaded ratchet. This ensures that winding is possible in one direction only thereby safeguarding the movement from damage caused by accidental reverse winding. It is also called a Tipsy Key.

Breguet Overcoil - A flat spiral balance spring whose inner end is bent inward and whose outer end is bent up and across the coil. Breguet used flat springs to keep his watches slim but bent them thus to achieve isochronism.

Bull's-Eye Glass - A flattened dome glass with the center ground flat. It was popular during the second half of the eighteenth century.

Caliber - A term originally used to denote design and size of a movement, but it has since developed a broader meaning and can now include the name of the designer.

Cannon Pinion - See Motion Work.

Center Pinion - See Train.

Center Seconds - A seconds hand that is pivoted at the center of the dial. It is sometimes referred to as a sweep seconds hand.

Center Wheel - See Train.

Châtelaine - An elaborate and ornate chain for suspending a ladies watch. The decoration usually matches that of the watch case. Provision is made on the chain to suspend the watch key and at least one trinket. An example can be seen in Fig. 68 on page 000 and in Color Plate I.

Chronograph - A conventional watch with additional mechanism that enables a center seconds hand to be started, stopped and returned to zero (twelve o'clock position) by means of a push-piece or slide. The number of complete revolutions (minutes) is recorded on a subsidiary dial. The action does not interfere with the time train.

Chronometer - Originally a watch or portable marine clock fitted with a detent escapement. Now a term more loosely used by European makers when referring to any timepiece that has been awarded a rating certificate by the authorities at the Neuchâtel or Geneva observatory.

Chronoscope - A watch fitted with a Wandering Hour Dial. See Chapter Four.

Click - A small pivoted lever or pawl whose tapered end engages between the teeth of a ratchet wheel. It is held in position by a light spring and allows the ratchet wheel to rotate in one direction only. The ratchet wheel is secured to the mainspring arbor, and when the spring is wound, the ratchet teeth escape past the click. When winding tension is removed the click prevents backward rotation of the mainspring arbor.

Clock-Watch - A watch that strikes each hour at the appropriate time. It is automatic in action and is not to be confused with a Repeater.

Cock - A half bridge piece, one end of which is secured to the movement plate, and the other end of which is drilled to receive the top pivot of an arbor. It was originally used to support the balance. When the Lepine caliber was introduced in about 1770 each wheel had its own cock. Early European watches were fitted with a cock that completely spanned the balance and had a foot at each end. These are known as bridge cocks. Between 1600 and 1750 cocks went through many changes so they can be useful guides to the age of a movement. See Chapter Two and Chapter Four.

Compensation Balance - A balance that overcomes the adverse effects of temperature changes by its own automatic compensation. A watch without a compensation balance loses when the temperature rises and gains as the temperature drops.

It was Pierre Le Roy who, in 1776, first introduced a balance with temperature compensation. He was followed by other makers with a variety of ideas until, in 1782, Thomas Earnshaw produced the cut bimetallic balance we know today. See Chapter Six.

Compensation Curb - The earliest form of temperature compensation in which a Bimetallic device was used. One end of the strip is fixed, and the other end carries two index pins between which passes the outer end of the balance spring. When the temperature rises or falls, the strip bends one way or the other moving the pins along the balance spring and thus decreasing or increasing the effective length of the spring; shortening the spring produces a gain, and vice versa.

Another method was to make the strip U-shaped. One end is fixed and the free end carries an index pin. Close to the free end of the strip is an immovable index pin, and between the pins passes the outer end of the spring. Changes in temperature vary the distance between the pins allowing the spring more or less freedom which has the effect of altering the length of the spring.

Complicated Work - Mechanisms that are additional to the time and strike, e.g. repeat, calendar and chronograph work.

Consular Case - A watch case named after Napoleon and introduced when he was Consul of France. When the hinged back is opened it reveals an immovable inner back that has two holes, one for winding and the other for setting the hands. At the front is a hinged glass bezel which, when opened, permits the movement to swing out of the case on its own hinge. When the case is closed, the back and the bezel meet and no part of the body is visible.

Contrate Wheel - A toothed wheel with teeth at right angles to its plane. It is used to drive the escape wheel pinion in a verge escapement.

Coqueret - A steel end-plate screwed to the balance cock to support the top pivot of the balance staff. The bearing face is highly polished. It was introduced in France in about 1735. By 1770 it was in general use in France for good quality watches and continued to be until the end of the century when the English released their secret knowledge of jewelling.

Count Wheel - A flat disc that performs as a wheel in the striking train. Eleven notches are cut in its edge at progressively increasing distances. A pivoted L-shaped arm rests with its short arm in one of the notches. When it is time for the watch to strike, the arm is raised clear of the wheel and the strike train is released. The count wheel slowly turns and with each strike the arm is raised and then allowed to drop back onto the edge of the wheel. Striking continues until the arm drops into the following notch and the strike train is halted. At one o'clock the arm is raised and drops back into the same notch, hence only eleven notches around the count wheel. The disadvantage of the system is that it strikes progressively regardless of the position of the hands.

Crown Wheel Escapement - An alternative name for Verge Escapement.

Curb Pins - Two pins attached to the index or regulator. Between the pins passes the outer end of the balance spring. Turning the index or regulator repositions the pins in relation to the balance spring. Moving the pins towards the outer end increases the effective length of the spring and slows the watch, and moving the pins towards the center has the reverse effect.

A similar result, but to a lesser extent, is achieved by altering the distance between the pins. Increasing the distance increases the effective length and slows down the watch, whereas decreasing the distance decreases the length and speeds up the watch.

Cylinder Escapement - A horizontal dead beat escapement developed by George Graham in 1726 from an invention by Thomas Tompion in 1695. The main body of the balance staff is a cylinder with a little more than half its diameter removed from its lower end. It is in this cavity that the escape wheel teeth operate. The teeth are triangular and mounted on short pins secured at right angles to the face of the wheel. A tooth rests against the outside face of the revolving cylinder until the cut-away portion presents itself. When the two are in line the tooth enters the cylinder and in so doing gives an impulse to the entry lip of the cylinder. At the completion of its swing the balance changes direction and the tooth is allowed to escape. As it does so, it gives a second impulse, this time to the exit lip and in the reverse direction. This escapement proved to be superior to the verge escapement. See Chapter Four.

Dead Beat Escapement - Any escapement that has no Recoil. The cylinder escapement is an example.

Debaufre Escapement - An escapement invented by Peter Debaufre in 1704. Whether watches fitted with it have survived is unknown. It is a dead beat escapement and the first of the frictional rest escapements. See Ormskirk Escapement and Chapter Four.

Deck Watch - A large accurate watch, too big to be worn and usually supplied in a box, for conveying the time of a marine chronometer to parts of the ship.

Detached Escapement - An escapement in which the balance is permitted to operate almost completely free from any influence of the time train. Examples are Detent and Lever.

Detent Escapement - An escapement invented by Pierre Le Roy in 1748 for use at sea in marine timekeepers. It was the first detached escapement ever to be made and the first in which the balance was able to swing almost completely free from any mechanical interference. Le Roy called it his detent escapement. By 1766 the design was much improved and it was tested at sea on the ship ''Aurore.'' Its performance was equal to that of Harrison's No. 4.

Four years later, in 1770, John Arnold invented his own form of detent escapement in which the detent functioned on a pivot. It was not a success and Arnold eventually abandoned his pivoted detent in favor of Thomas Earnshaw's spring detent.

The spring detent escapement, invented by Earnshaw in 1780, was so named because the detent was mounted on a spring. It was a great success and, in a more sophisticated form, is now used internationally in marine chronometers.

A detent escapement is extremely delicate and highly accurate. See Chapter Five.

Draw - A safety action that takes place in a lever escapement. The locking faces of the escape wheel teeth and the pallet stones are cut at such angles that when pressed together the pallet stone is drawn into deeper engagement with the escape wheel until the lever is held against one or the other of the two banking pins. This action creates imperceptible recoil and takes place when the balance is swinging through its supplementary arc. Without draw, the lever could be jolted from the banking pin causing the guard pin of the fork to contact the roller and create friction. It was invented by John Leroux in 1785. See Chapter Six.

Dumb Repeater - See Repeater.

Duplex Escapement - A very delicate frictional rest escapement that produces an impulse in one direction only. It is related to the cylinder escapement and is capable of giving an excellent performance. It was introduced in about 1750 by Pierre Le Roy but was never really popular with the French makers. The English used it during the first half of the nineteenth century in their high grade watches in preference to the lever escapement. See Chapter Six.

Dust Cap - A brass cover that fits over the movement to keep out dirt and dust. The caps are confined mostly to English watches with movements that are hinged to the case. They were introduced in about 1715 and continued in use until the early nineteenth century.

End-Plate - A flat metal disc screwed to a plate or cock to cover a pivot hole and provide a bearing surface for the end of the pivot. Without an end-plate the end thrust would be taken by the shoulder on the pivot.

Endstone - An end-plate made of a precious stone or jewel. Usually fitted to the balance cock.

Engine Turning - A method of light engraving carried out on a lathe. It produces a variety of repetitive designs and was used to decorate the backs of watch cases. Also known as Guilloché.

Escape Pinion - See Train.

Escape Wheel - The last wheel in the time train. It is alternately locked and released, one tooth at a time, and it is from these teeth, directly or indirectly depending on the type of escapement, that the balance receives its impulses. See also Train.

Escapement - The mechanism fitted between the time train and the balance. Its function is to control the release of motive power, stored in the mainspring, by allowing it to be expended through the time train in equal amounts. The escapement also imparts impulses to the spring balance to keep it in swinging motion; this oscillation of the balance ensures the measured amounts of energy from the mainspring are released at regular intervals.

Many different escapements have been designed but they all fall into one of two classifications, i.e. Frictional Rest or Detached.

Farthing - The lowest denomination of currency in Great Britain before the introduction of the decimal system in 1971.

Five-Minute Repeater - See Repeater.

Floating Hour Dial - See Wandering Hour Dial.

Foliot - The earliest form of escapement controller. It is a horizontal bar with a fixed weight at each end, rather like a dumbbell in appearance, and is mounted centrally on the upper end of a verge. It was mostly used on early German Stackfreed watches and confined to the sixteenth century.

Fork - The fork-shaped end of the lever in a lever escapement which receives the Ruby Pin on the balance staff roller.

Form Watch - A pendant watch made to look like one of a variety of irrelevant objects. Some typical examples are a skull, bird, six-pointed star, cross or shell. They were popular among European makers during the first half of the seventeenth century and then went out of fashion about 1665. Early in the nineteenth century they reappeared in Switzerland and have remained popular ever since.

Four-Color Gold - Gold that has been mixed with alloys to produce tints of yellow, silvery-white, red and green. It was introduced in about 1770 and remained popular as a form of decorating cases and dials for about one hundred years.

Fourth Pinion - See Train.

Fourth Wheel - See Train.

Frame - The Top Plate and Bottom Plate.

Free-Sprung - A term describing a balance spring free from the influence of curb pins. Isochronous springs are not usually fitted with regulators because the effect of the curb pins destroys isochronism in the spring. Such springs are fitted to marine chronometers and top quality pocket watches, and regulation is carried out before fitting. Any final adjustment is made by turning timing screws in the rim of the balance.

Frictional Rest Escapement - An escapement in which the escape wheel teeth are locked by resting against some part of the balance. Friction is present during the Supplementary Arc thus preventing the balance from oscillating with freedom. For this reason a frictional rest escapement is inferior to a Detached Escapement. Examples are duplex, virgule, verge and cylinder.

Full Plate - A top plate that completely covers the movement. All wheels are therefore supported between the top and bottom plates. The balance and balance cock are positioned on the outside of the top plate. See also Half Plate and Three-Quarter Plate.

Fusee - A method of providing the time train with a constant driving force no matter whether the mainspring is fully wound or partially expended. It consists of a spirally grooved cone mounted on the great wheel arbor and is connected to the spring barrel by a length of gut or chain. See Chapter One.

Going Barrel - See Barrel and Train.

Going Fusee - A fusee fitted with Maintaining Power. See also Train.

Gong - A length of wire coiled in a flat spiral and fitted to repeaters and striking watches instead of a bell. It was probably introduced by Julien Le Roy.

Grande Sonnerie - A refinement of quarter-hour striking. With each quarter hour is included the previous hour.

Great Wheel - The first and largest wheel in a time train. It is part of the Fusee or Going Barrel.

Guilloché - See Engine Turning.

Hairspring - The common name for Balance Spring.

Half Plate - A top plate that is little more than semi-circular in shape. It is drilled to accept the upper pivots of the going barrel, or barrel and fusee, the center wheel and the third wheel. In the cut-away area, the fourth wheel, escape wheel and balance are supported by their own cocks screwed to the bottom plate.

Half-Quarter Repeater - See Repeater.

Hallmark - The Assay mark that is punched on gold and silver. See Appendix Three.

Hand-Setting - In the earliest watches, moving the single hour hand to the correct time with one's finger. When minute hands were added, one set the watch by turning a key on the squared end of the arbor carrying the hands. Later, when Keyless Winding was introduced, the winding button was used for hand-setting. See also Motion Work.

Hanging Barrel - A going barrel that is supported at the upper end of the arbor only.

Helical Spring - A spring that is formed by being wound around a rod. Almost all marine chronometer balance springs are helical in shape.

Horizontal Escapement - An alternative, but little used, name for Cylinder Escapement.

Hour Wheel - See Train.

Hunter - A type of watch that has a case with a hinged cover completely enclosing the glass for protection. The cover is opened by a push-piece. A half-hunter or demi-hunter has a hole in the center of the cover to enable the hands to be seen. Sometimes a pebble glass is fitted to the hole to provide some small magnification. It is said that Napoleon I took a knife and cut a hole in the front cover of his watch; hence a half-hunter is frequently called a Napoleon watch.

Impulse - Mainspring energy that is conveyed to the balance by the time train and escapement to keep the balance in swinging motion. For example, the escape wheel teeth of a Cylinder Escapement give the cylinder an impulse in one direction when they enter the cylinder, and in the opposite direction when they escape.

Impulse Pin - A pin that is fitted to the balance staff roller in a lever escapement and functions in the fork of the lever. When the pin enters the fork, the lever is moved sideways on its pivot and an escape wheel tooth is released. The escaping tooth gives an impulse to the pallet and so to the lever fork and impulse pin causing the balance to swing. Impulse pins on early watches are made of ruby or sapphire and are sometimes called ruby pins.

Index - The regulator in a watch. A lever that pivots horizontally on the balance cock concentric with the balance. One end carries two Curb Pins for altering the effective length of the balance spring, and the other end moves across a scale marked at one end F or A (fast or advancer), and at the other end S or R (slow or retarder).

Isochronous - Functioning at regular intervals. A balance is said to be isochronous if the time taken for each oscillation remains constant no matter whether the arc of swing increases or decreases. To achieve this, or very nearly achieve this, makers fitted isochronous springs. Ordinary spiral or helical springs do not possess the property of isochronism but in 1782 John Arnold found that a helical spring became isochronous if the ends were turned inward. Similarly, Breguet's overcoil enabled makers to produce isochronous flat spiral springs.

Jewel - See Endstone.

Jump-Hour - An hour hand that remains stationary for an hour and then, on the hour, jumps forward to the next hour. It was frequently fitted by Breguet to his repeater watches.

Keyless Winding - The use of the pendant to wind the mainspring - a method first introduced in 1793 by Robert Leslie. During the first quarter of the nineteenth century a number of variations were used but they all relied upon pulling out or pushing in the pendant, an action that became known as pump winding. See Chapter Six.

Lepine Caliber - A movement with no top plate; each wheel is supported by its own bar, bridge or cock. It is sometimes referred to as a barred movement. The arrangement was introduced by Jean-Antoine Lepine in about 1770.

Lever Escapement - One of the first escapements with a detached balance. It was invented by Thomas Mudge in 1754 and most probably by Julien Le Roy, quite independently, at about the same time. There are two basic types, the English lever and the European lever. The principles of operation are the same but the layouts differ. The use of the European or Swiss lever eventually became universal. See Chapter Six.

Lodestone - Magnetic iron ore.

Maintaining Power - A device composed of a spring-loaded ratchet and click which John Harrison fitted to his fusees; this allowed the great wheel to drive the time train without interruption during winding. When a fusee watch without maintaining power is wound, the fusee is turned in the reverse direction, power from the mainspring is removed from the time train, and the watch stops. This problem does not apply to a movement with a going barrel. See Chapter Five.

Marine Chronometer - A mechanical and portable timekeeper of great accuracy used at sea for the purpose of calculating the longitude of a ship's position. Early chronometers were all fitted with Detent Escapements, but in later years the term came to mean any timepiece used at sea capable of maintaining the accuracy required. See Chapter Five.

Middle Temperature Error - The rate of error between the two temperatures at which a bimetallic compensation balance is accurate, the balance not maintaining accurate timekeeping throughout the normal temperature range. Fitting a secondary compensator frequently corrects such error.

Minute Repeater - See Repeater.

Montre à Répétition - Repeater watch made by Breguet. See Chapter Seven.

Montre à Souscription - Good quality plain watch made by Breguet in batches to keep down the cost of manufacture. Members of the public remitted an advance payment when ordering such a watch.

Montre à Tact - A watch with a stout steel hand mounted centrally on the case back, and twelve touch pieces secured equidistantly around the rim of the case representing hour positions. By feeling the hand and the touch pieces in the dark one could approximate the time.

Montre Mixtes - Watch made under Breguet's supervision but not in his workshop. See Chapter Seven.

Moon Hand - See Breguet Hand.

Motion Work - The Train of wheels that is between the dial and the bottom plate and carries the hour hand. See Fig. 82.

Movement - Most easily described as a watch without its case, dial and hands.

Musical Watch - Introduced in Switzerland at the end of the eighteenth century, a watch whose mechanism consists of a flat pinned disc that rotates beneath a row of graduated music springs. The mechanism is fitted between the dial and the bottom plate. Some watches have pinned cylinders but these are rare. The musical watch was very popular during the first half of the nineteenth century. The mechanism prompted the idea of musical snuff boxes, and then, during the reign of Queen Victoria, was applied to musical boxes.

Oignon - The colloquial name for bulbous-shaped French watches of the late seventeenth and early eighteenth centuries; so called because of their resemblance to an onion.

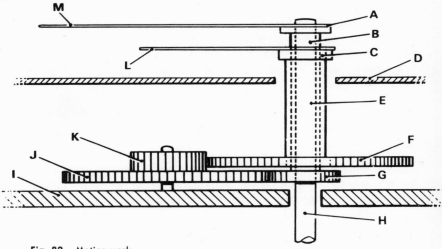

Fig. 82. Motion work.

(A) Minute hand boss	(H) Center wheel arbor
(B) Cannon pinion pipe	(I) Top plate
(C) Hour hand boss	(J) Minute wheel
(D) Dial	(K) Minute wheel pinion
(E) Hour wheel pipe	(L) Hour hand
(F) Hour wheel	(M) Minute hand
(G) Cannon pinion	

Oil Sink - An oil reservoir produced by countersinking the outer end of a pivot hole in a movement plate. It was introduced in 1715 by Julien Le Roy and Henry Sully but not generally used until the second half of the eighteenth century.

Ormskirk Escapement - Watches made with a form of Debaufre Escapement during the early nineteenth century in the town of Ormskirk in Lancashire, England.

Overcoil - See Breguet Overcoil.

Pair-Case - An outer case which holds and protects the case of the watch proper. When the outer case is shut the watch is completely enclosed. Pair-cases were introduced about 1630 and were very popular in England and in Europe. English makers continued using them until early in the nineteenth century. See Chapter Two.

Pallet - The parts of a lever escapement that successively lock and release the teeth of the escape wheel; they are known as the entry pallet and the exit pallet respectively. Each time a tooth escapes from a pallet it imparts an impulse to that pallet. See Chapter Six.

Pantograph - A jointed framework of rods for copying drawings on the same, or different, scale.

Parechute - An anti-shock device, invented by Breguet about 1793, for the protection of balance staff pivots. The balance staff endstones are supported by short lengths of very light spring steel. It was the first anti-shock device ever used.

Pendant - The tubular neck which is attached to the top of a case and carries the Bow. In keyless watches the pendant carries the winding button and stem.

Pendulum - Actually a simple arrangement for a false or mock pendulum which is seen swinging behind an aperture cut in the dial, or is visible through an opening in the balance cock or bridge. See Chapter Four.

Perpetual Calendar - A calendar watch that automatically adjusts itself to the varying number of days in the months and also corrects itself at leap years.

Perpetual Watch - A method of winding by means of a swinging weight that is set in motion by the movements of the wearer. The

English claimed that it was invented in 1780 by Louis Recordon, a Swiss watchmaker living in England, but it is now generally accepted that the idea was introduced by a Swiss watchmaker, John Perrelet, in about 1770. Even so, it was Breguet who first applied the idea and his now famous montres perpétuelles are evidence enough of the success of the invention.

Since those days there have been many variations but the one most favored in modern watches is the completely rotating weight. The perpetual watch is also called pedometer-winding, self-winding and automatic.

Pillar Plate - See Bottom Plate.

Pillars - The distance pieces that hold the movement plates in their relative positions. During the first three hundred years of watchmaking, movement pillars were very ornate. They were fixed to the bottom plate and pinned to the top plate. See Figs. 21a and 21b.

Pinion - The smaller of two wheels mounted on the same arbor. There are usually six teeth which are called leaves.

Pinwork - See Piqué.

Piqué - A form of decoration using gold and silver pins or studs to produce designs on the outside of shell and leather cases. It was a popular method of decorating pair-cases. See Chapter Eight.

Pivoted Detent - Sometimes called a Bascule. See also Detent Escapement.

Pivots - The turned down ends of an arbor. They support the weight of the arbor and its associated wheel and pinion, and their reduced diameters are located in pivot holes drilled in jewels.

Poker Hand - An English minute hand very popular during the eighteenth century. Slender and slightly tapered, it was used with a Beetle Hand to point the hour.

Potence - A bracket that is screwed to a movement plate and drilled to accept one pivot of an arbor.

Pulse Piece - See Repeater.

Pump Winding - See Keyless Winding.

Puritan Watch - A small English watch usually silver, oval in shape and without any form of decoration. It was made during the second quarter of the seventeenth century.

Quarter Repeater - See Repeater.

Quarter Screws - See Timing Screws.

Rack Lever Escapement - An escapement in which the pivoted lever has a rack at one end that engages with a pinion mounted on the balance staff. The balance is thereby made to swing through a large arc of at least two complete revolutions. See Chapter Four.

Recoil - Very slight backward rotation of the escape wheel caused by a pallet pressing against an escape wheel tooth immediately after locking.

Regulator - A device for altering the rate of a watch. The earliest watches were usually fitted with one of two forms of regulators: In German stackfreed watches the foliot banked against two hog bristles during its oscillation. By adjusting the distance between the two bristles the watchmaker could adjust the arc of swing of the foliot. In French fusee watches the maker effected regulation by using a ratchet for the Set-up of the mainspring. Winding the mainspring in its fully run down condition removed some of the residual tension. This method was in use up to about 1640. See Chapter One.

About 1625 a new method of setting up the mainspring was introduced. In place of the ratchet, a worm and wheel were used. They were mounted on the top plate and turning a key on the squared end of the worm accomplished setting up. See Chapter Two.

After balance springs were introduced, Tompion devised his own form of regulator. He used a toothed segment beneath the balance spring. One end of the segment carried two curb pins that embraced the outer coil of the balance spring. The other end was geared to a small wheel mounted on a square-ended arbor. Tompion effected regulation by turning the arbor with a key which caused the curb pins to move along the balance spring and alter its effective length.

Another form of regulator that was introduced about the same time was a worm and slide. The worm was mounted on the top plate and operated a slide that carried two curb pins along the outer coil of the balance spring. Credit for this invention is given to Nathaniel Barrow. See Chapter Four.

In 1755 Joseph Bosley introduced a regulator in the form of a lever that he fitted beneath the balance cock. The lever was pivoted, and on the short arm were two curb pins between which passed the outer coil of the balance spring. The long arm, which moved the regulator, passed over a scale engraved in the top plate. This was the forerunner of the modern Index regulator which is positioned on top of the balance cock.

Regulator Clock - An instrument whose function is to provide accurate time and nothing else. It is essentially a precision instrument. The eight-day movement is fitted with a time train only. There is no strike mechanism or any form of complicated work, and so, strictly speaking, it is a timepiece and not a clock.

A regulator clock is built into a tall-case rather like a grandfather clock and is controlled by a compensated pendulum and driven by weights. It always has a dead beat or detached form of escapement, never a recoil.

To avoid the use of under-dial motion work the clockmaker arranges the hands with the minute hand in the center of the dial, the seconds hand above and the hour hand below, each with its own dial markings.

Remontoire - A device that is used when the balance spring is not isochronous. It is a light spring that is kept wound by the time train and is used to drive the escape wheel. By this method a more constant driving force is produced. If the watchmaker uses the spring to drive the balance by interposing it between the escape wheel and the balance, the arrangement is known as a remontoire escapement.

Repeater - A watch that strikes the approximate time on bells or gongs, but only when the time is selected. Moving a slide in the edge of the case winds the repeat mechanism spring and sets the strike in motion. It is usual for hours to be struck on a low note, minutes on a high note, and quarters on a double note (ting-tang). A few repeater watches are fitted with chime mechanism. The repeater was introduced by Daniel Quare in about 1680.

Quarter Repeater. A watch that strikes the hour and the number of quarters past the hour. For example, for twenty minutes to four o'clock three single strokes are followed by two ting-tangs.

Half-Quarter Repeater. A watch that strikes hours, quarters and midway, or more, towards the next quarter. For example, for twenty-five minutes past nine o'clock nine single strokes, one ting-tang and one single stroke sound. This arrangement was introduced late in the seventeenth century.

Minute Repeater. A watch that strikes the hours, quarters and the number of minutes past the last quarter. For example, for nine minutes to eleven o'clock ten single strokes are followed by three ting-tangs and six single strokes. These repeaters first appeared during the last quarter of the eighteenth century but one hundred years elapsed before they were made in any quantity.

Five-Minute Repeater. In addition to the hours and quarters, this mechanism strikes for each five-minute period that has elapsed since the hour or since the last quarter. For example, for eighteen minutes to two o'clock one single stroke, two ting-tangs and two single strokes sound. These watches first appeared about 1710 but eighteenth century five minute repeaters are rare.

Dumb Repeater. A repeating watch that has no gong or bell. The hammer strikes the case, or a metal block, but the blow can be felt rather than heard. The watch was introduced in about 1750 by Julien Le Roy. Sometimes the movement is fitted with a pin called the pulse piece. This pin protrudes through a hole in the edge of the case and by placing one's finger against the pin while the watch is striking one can feel the hammer blows quite distinctly.

Ruby Cylinder - The cylinder in a cylinder escapement which is made of ruby instead of steel. It was greatly favored by Breguet.

Ruby Pin - See Impulse Pin.

Set-up - The partial winding of the mainspring before engaging it with the train, a practice that was usual before balance springs were introduced. This removed some of the residual tension and resulted in more even torque. The partial winding of the spring in a going barrel was carried out before the stop work was fitted, and in a fusee watch the winding was done before the gut or chain was wound on to the fusee. When applied to a pre-balance spring watch with fusee, the set-up was used as a form of Regulator.

Six-Hour Dial - A rare late seventeenth century dial. It has a single hand that sweeps the dial once in six hours. Arabic numerals 7 to 12 are superimposed on Roman numerals I to VI. There are only six hour positions and the space between them is enough to divide the minute ring legibly into two minute divisions. See Chapter Four.

Stackfreed - An inferior arrangement fitted to sixteenth century German watches to compensate for the irregular force produced by mainsprings during unwinding. See Chapter One.

Stop Work - A device to prevent over-winding of a mainspring. It also makes possible the Set-up of a spring.

Sugar Tongs - A compensation curb, designed by Thomas Earnshaw that consisted of two bimetallic strips placed parallel to one another and fixed to a plate at one end. The two free ends each carried a pin between which passed the outer end of the balance spring. Any variation of temperature caused the two pins to move closer together or further apart thereby altering the effective length of the spring.

Sun and Moon Dial - A popular seventeenth century dial with a conventional minute hand and minute ring. The hour hand is replaced by a revolving disc behind a semi-circular opening in the upper half of the dial. The semi-circle is divided into twelve hours and is marked with Roman numerals. The disc, which revolves once in every twenty-four hours, is decorated with the sun and the moon positioned diametrically opposite one another. During the hours of darkness the moon indicates the hour between 6 p.m. and 6 a.m., and during the day the sun moves round the semi-circle from 6 a.m. to 6 p.m. See Chapter Four.

Supplementary Arc - That portion of the total oscillating arc that is described by a balance between the moment after impulse is complete until immediately prior to unlocking.

Sweep Seconds - See Center Seconds.

Temperature Compensation - The use of any method that maintains regular timekeeping throughout variations of temperature. The most widely used were a Compensation Balance and Compensation Curb. See Chapter Six.

Terminal Curves - The shaped ends of a balance spring. Shaping the ends makes the spring Isochronous and one of the essential requirements of an escapement that is to achieve good timekeeping. It was found that if a spring could be arranged so that its center of gravity lay on the axis of the balance, isochronism existed. To achieve this, the end coils of springs were bent inward. In the case of a Helical Spring the two end coils were straightened and bent inward; with a flat spiral spring the inner end was bent inward and the outer end was bent up and inward. This latter is known as a Breguet Overcoil, so named for the man who invented it.

Third Pinion - See Train.

Third Wheel - See Train.

Three-Quarter Plate - A Top Plate that is about three-quarters the size of a Full Plate for the same Caliber. Pivot holes are provided for the going barrel, or barrel and fusee arrangement, the center wheel, the third wheel and the fourth wheel. In the cut-away area are the escape wheel and the balance with their separate cocks.

Timing Screws - Sometimes referred to as quarter screws. They are positioned in the balance rim ninety degrees from one another (see Fig. 65 on page 153). Unscrewing them slows down the rate, and turning them inward speeds up the rate. It is usual to divide the amount of adjustment equally between two opposite screws in order to maintain the poise of the balance.

Tipsy Key - See Breguet Key.

Top Plate - The plate furthest from the dial.

Torque - The turning moment of a tangential force.

Touch Pins - Pins found in sixteenth century watches. They were inserted at the hour markings on the dial to assist in determining the time in darkness.

Tourbillon - Breguet's regulateur à tourbillon, a device to eliminate vertical position timing errors. He accomplished this by mounting the escapement on a continuously rotating platform. See Chapter Seven.

Train - A number of toothed wheels and pinions that are geared together and transmit mechanical energy from one component to another. For example, the time train links the mainspring barrel or fusee with the escapement, and the strike train conveys energy to the hammer. Fig. 83 illustrates the formation of a time train. The minute hand is mounted on the end of the center wheel arbor, the seconds hand is on the fourth wheel arbor, and the escape wheel teeth provide the impulses necessary to maintain the balance in oscillation. The hour hand is driven by the Motion Work which is not part of the time train.

235

Verge Escapement - Sometimes referred to as a crown wheel escapement it dates back to the thirteenth century and was the only escapement in use in mediaeval clocks. It was still the only escapement when watches were introduced at the beginning of the sixteenth century. This situation remained until new escapements were introduced following the inventions of the clock pendulum in 1657 and the watch balance spring in 1675. Even so, watches continued to be fitted with verge escapements as late as 1850.

The escapement consists of a crown wheel, driven by the time train, and a vertically mounted verge with two pallets that release the crown wheel one tooth at a time. Mounted on top of the verge is a balance. See Chapter One.

Virgule Escapement - A rare French escapement that was in use from about 1780 until approximately 1805. Its name is the French word for comma whose shape it closely resembles. It is sometimes referred to as the hook escapement, again because of its shape. Though invented by J.A. Lepaute, it was introduced by Jean Antoine.

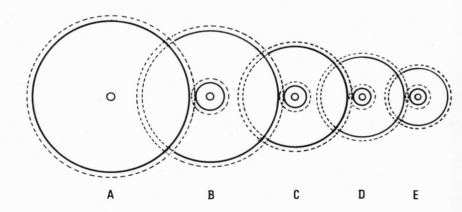

Fig. 83. Time train.
    (A) Going barrel or fusee
    (B) Center wheel and pinion (1 rev. per hr.)
    (C) Third wheel and pinion
    (D) Fourth wheel and pinion (1 rev. per hr.)
    (E) Escape wheel and pinion

The ends of the escape wheel teeth are upstanding, rather like pins, and they lock on the outside of the virgule cylinder. As the virgule rotates, each tooth enters the cylinder, then passes along the inner face of the virgule tail and gives impulse as it escapes.

It is a frictional rest escapement and impulse is imparted in one direction only. See Chapter Six.

Wandering Hour Dial - An alternative name is floating hour dial, and watches fitted with these dials are sometimes called chronoscopes. They were fitted to Dutch, English and German watches from about 1675 until approximately 1720.

In the upper half of the dial is a semi-circular slot. Behind the slot is a rotating disc carrying a small window through which is visible a Roman hour numeral. The disc carries the numeral round the slot in one hour. The upper edge of the slot is marked in sixty minute divisions.

To read the time, one checks the hour shown by the numeral in the window, and the number of minutes past the hour from the minute scale. See Chapter Four.

Watch Paper - A disc of printed paper bearing the name and address of the watchmaker or repairer. The paper was used with pair-case watches and was inserted between the watch case and the pair-case. It served as an advertisement and as a protection against scratches on the watch case from chafing against the pair-case.

Winding Square - The squared end of the fusee or barrel arbor over which one places the key when winding the watch.

Dates of Interest

1470 First spring-driven clocks produced in Italy.

1475 Fusee introduced in Italy.

1500 Spring-driven drum-shaped table clocks introduced in Germany.

1505 First watches made by Peter Henlein of Nuremberg, Germany.

1510 Stackfreed introduced in Germany.

1518 Beginning of French watchmaking.

1523 Brass used in France.

1550 Introduction of screws for use in metal.

1575 Wheel balance introduced.

1580 Brass used in Germany.

1600 First watchmakers in London.

1600 Form watches appeared in France, Germany and Switzerland.

1601 Rock crystal cases introduced.

1610 Painted enamel cases introduced in Limoges, France.

1630 Watch glasses first used.

1630 Puritan watches appeared.

1630 First pair-cases used.

1660 Snap-in bezels for glasses introduced.

1660 Fusee chains in use.

1667 Founding of the Royal Society in London.

1672 Wheel-cutting machine invented by Dr. Robert Hooke.

1675 Balance spring invented by Christiaan Huygens.

1675 Royal Observatory founded at Greenwich, London.

1675 Introduction of pocket watch coincident with arrival of men's waistcoats.

1675 All-white enamel dials appeared.

1676	Rack striking invented by Edward Barlow.
1676	Motion work and minute hand introduced by Daniel Quare.
1677	"Pendulum" watches appeared.
1678	English hallmarking of gold cases began.
1680	Four-wheel time trains introduced in London.
1680	Repeat mechanism invented by Daniel Quare.
1695	Cylinder escapement invented by Thomas Tompion, Edward Barlow and William Houghton.
1704	Jewelling for pivots introduced.
1704	First frictional rest escapement invented by Peter Debaufre.
1710	Dust caps for movements first used.
1715	Oil sinks invented by Henry Sully.
1720	English hallmarking of silver cases began.
1722	Rack lever escapement invented by the Abbé de Hautefeuille.
1725	Improved cylinder escapement invented by George Graham.
1725	Adjustable potence invented by Julien Le Roy.
1734	Maintaining power invented by John Harrison.
1734	First bimetallic compensator invented by John Harrison.
1748	Pivoted detent escapement invented by Pierre Le Roy.
1750	White enamel dials in general use.
1750	Duplex escapement introduced by Pierre Le Roy.
1750	Center seconds hand introduced.
1754	Detached lever escapement invented by Thomas Mudge.
1756	Bimetallic compensation curb invented by John Harrison.
1764	Ruby cylinder escapement introduced.
1766	First compensation balance (alcohol and mercury) invented by Pierre Le Roy.
1775	First appearance of makers' names on English enamel dials.
1776	Helical balance spring invented by John Arnold.
1780	Spring detent escapement invented by Thomas Earnshaw.
1780	Virgule escapement introduced by Jean Antoine.
1780	Automatic winding invented by Abraham-Louis Perrelet of Switzerland.
1780	First bimetallic balance invented by John Arnold.
1782	Isochronism introduced by John Arnold.
1785	Draw applied to lever escapement by John Leroux.
1791	Rack lever escapement popularized by Peter Litherland.
1793	Pump winding introduced by Robert Leslie.
1801	Tourbillon escapement invented by Abraham-Louis Breguet.
1820	Keyless winding introduced by Thomas Prest.

Crowned Heads of England

Accession	Monarch	Died	House	Remarks
1046	Edward the Confessor	1066		Founded Westminster Abbey
1066	Harold	1066		Killed at Battle of Hastings. End of Anglo-Saxon reign
1066	William I (The Conqueror)	1087		Compiled Doomsday Book. Built Tower of London
1087	William II (William Rufus)	1100		Mysteriously killed whilst hunting in the New Forest
1100	Henry I	1135		
1135	Stephen	1154		
1154	Henry II	1189		
1189	Richard I	1199	Plantagenet	
1199	John	1216	''	
1216	Henry III	1272	''	
1272	Edward I	1307	''	
1307	Edward II	1327	''	Murdered
1327	Edward III	1377	''	
1377	Richard II	1400	''	Dethroned 1399. Murdered
1399	Henry IV	1413	Lancaster	
1413	Henry V	1422	''	
1422	Henry VI	1471	''	Deposed 1461
1461	Edward IV	1483	York	
1483	Edward V	1483	''	Murdered
1483	Richard III	1485	''	Slain at Battle of Bosworth

End of the Middle Ages

1485	Henry VII	1509	Tudor	
1509	Henry VIII	1547	''	
1547	Edward VI	1553	''	
1553	Lady Jane Grey	1554	''	Beheaded. Reigned 9 days during 1553
1553	Mary	1558	Tudor	
1558	Elizabeth I	1603	''	
1603	James I	1625	Stuart	James VI of Scotland
1625	Charles I	1649	''	Beheaded
1649	Commonwealth	1658		Oliver Cromwell, Protector
1658	''			Richard Cromwell, Protector Resigned 1660
1660	Charles II	1685	Stuart	
1685	James II	1701	''	Abdicated 1688
1688	William III and Mary (Prince of Orange)	1702	''	Mary died in 1694
1702	Anne	1714	''	
1714	George I	1727	Hanover	
1727	George II	1760	''	
1760	George III	1820	''	
1820	George IV	1830	''	
1830	William IV	1837	''	
1837	Victoria	1901	''	
1901	Edward VII	1910	''	
1910	George V	1936	Windsor	
1936	Edward VIII		''	Abdicated. (Duke of Windsor)
1936	George VI	1952	''	
1952	Elizabeth II		''	

Rulers of France

Accession	Monarch	Died	Remarks
1515	Francis I	1547	Invaded Italy
1547	Henri II	1559	Murdered
1559	Francis II	1560	Married Mary Stuart (Queen of Scots)
1560	Charles IX	1574	
1574	Henri III	1589	Murdered

1589	Henri IV	1610	Murdered
1610	Louis XIII	1643	
1643	Louis XIV	1715	
1715	Louis XV	1774	
1774	Louis XVI	1792	He and his wife Marie Antoinette guillotined during French Revolution
1792	Louis XVII	1795	Disappeared
1804	Napoleon Bonaparte (Emperor)	1814	Abdicated
1814	Louis XVIII	1824	
1824	Charles X	1830	Abdicated
1830	Louis Phillipe I	1848	
1848	Republic	1852	
1852	Napoleon III	1870	

English Hallmarks

IN 1300, during the reign of Edward I, the Worshipful Company of Goldsmiths was formed in London, and hallmarking was introduced to protect the public from the sale of inferior gold and silver wares.

The marks are of considerable interest to collectors of watches because they positively identify the year that a gold or silver watch case was submitted for assay. Providing the movement has not been re-cased, the age of a watch is determined with little difficulty.

Pure gold and silver are too soft for general use so they have to be alloyed with other metals. It is not possible to tell by appearance just how much precious metal is contained in these alloys and therefore, the British Government laid down certain standards of quality to which these metals must conform.

The assayer finds the precious metal content by removing small scrapings from the gold and silver ware and subjecting them to chemical analysis. If the metal conforms to one of the approved standards it is punch-marked with the appropriate hallmark. It is illegal in the United Kingdom to sell anything made of gold or silver unless it bears a hallmark.

King's Mark

At first, the leopard's head was the only mark to be used. It was known as the king's mark.

Maker's Mark

In 1363 a statute of Edward III provided that "every goldsmith should have a mark by himself, for which he should answer, to be

TOWN MARKS		
Gold and sterling silver	Brittania silver	LONDON
Gold and silver		EDINBURGH
Gold	Silver	SHEFFIELD
Gold	Silver	BIRMINGHAM
Gold and silver		DUBLIN
Gold and silver		CHESTER
Gold and silver		NEWCASTLE
Gold and silver		GLASGOW
Gold and silver		EXETER

struck beside the King's mark.'' For the next one hundred and fifteen years king's mark and maker's mark were used together. The early maker's marks were everyday objects such as a key, a bottle or a hammer. Later, the use of initials or the first two letters of the maker's name became compulsory.

Town Mark

When other assay offices were opened, the leopard's head was retained by London and new town marks appeared, as shown in the chart on page 244.

From time to time there were slight changes in the designs of the various emblems, and small alterations were made in the outlines of the surrounding shields.

There were also offices in Norwich and York, but today only London, Edinburgh, Sheffield and Birmingham are operating, all others having been closed.

Date Letter

In 1478, during the reign of Edward IV, a third mark was introduced to identify the year of assay. This mark took the form of a letter of the alphabet which was changed every year and became known as the date letter. Repetition has been avoided by employing different type and varying the shape of the surrounding shield. The chart on pages 246 and 247 shows the letters used by the London office since 1678 for marking silver ware. The same letters were used for gold but in some instances the shapes of the surrounding shields differed.

Standard Mark

In 1544, during the reign of Henry VIII, the wardens of the Goldsmiths' Company introduced the lion passant This was to indicate that the quality of gold and silver conformed to the required standard. Silver watch cases were rarely hallmarked before about 1720.

The chart on page 249 shows the different standard marks that have been used to denote the precious metal content of gold and silver alloy.

Note: 1 carat = 1/24, therefore 22 carat = 22/24 or 22 parts of fine gold and 2 parts alloy. The decimal mark indicates the minimum content of gold by weight in parts per thousand.

Year	Letter	Year	Letter	Year	Letter	Year	Letter	Year	Letter
1678	a	1707		1736	a	1765		1795	u
1679	b	1708		1737	b	1766		1796	A
1680	c	1709		1738	c	1767	m	1797	B
1681	d	1710		1739	d	1768		1798	C
1682	e	1711		1739	d	1769		1799	D
1683	f	1712		1740	e	1770	P	1800	E
1684	g	1713		1741	f	1771	Q	1801	F
1685	h	1714		1742	g	1772	R	1802	G
1686	i	1715		1743	h	1773	S	1803	H
1687	k	1716	A	1744	i	1774	T	1804	I
1688	l	1717	B	1745	k	1775	U	1805	K
1689	m	1718	C	1746	l	1776	a	1806	L
1690	n	1719	D	1747	m	1777	b	1807	M
1691	o	1720	E	1748	n	1778	c	1808	N
1692	p	1721	F	1749	o	1779	d	1809	O
1693	q	1722	G	1750	p	1780	e	1810	P
1694	r	1723	H	1751	q	1781	f	1811	Q
1695	s	1724	I	1752	r	1782	g	1812	R
1696	t	1725	K	1753	s	1783	h	1813	S
1697	a b	1726	L	1754	t	1784	i	1814	T
1698		1727	M	1755	u	1785	k	1815	U
1699		1728	N	1756	A	1786	l	1816	a
1700		1729	O	1757	B	1787	m	1817	b
1701	ff	1730	P	1758	C	1788	n	1818	C
1702		1731	Q	1759	D	1789	o	1819	d
1703		1732	R	1760	E	1790	p	1820	e
1704		1733	S	1761	F	1791	q	1821	f
1705		1734	T	1762	G	1792	r	1822	g
1706		1735	V	1763	H	1793	s	1823	h
				1764	I	1794	t	1824	i
								1825	k

Year	Letter	Year	Letter	Year	Letter	Year	Letter	Year	Letter
1826	l	1857	b	1890	P	1920	e	1950	P
1827	m	1858	c	1891	Q	1921	f	1951	Q
1828	n	1859	d	1892	R	1922	g	1952	R
1829	o	1860	e	1893	S	1923	h	1953	S
1830	p	1861	f	1894	T	1924	i	1954	T
1831	q	1862	g	1895	U	1925	k	1955	U
1832	r	1863	h	1896	a	1926	l	1956	a
1833	s	1864	i	1897	b	1927	m	1957	b
1834	t	1865	k	1898	c	1928	n	1958	c
1835	u	1866	l	1899	d	1929	o	1959	d
1836	A	1867	m	1900	e	1930	p	1960	e
1837	B	1868	n	1901	f	1931	q	1961	f
1838	C	1869	o	1902	g	1932	r	1962	g
1839	D	1870	p	1903	h	1933	s	1963	h
1840	E	1871	q	1904	i	1934	t	1964	i
1841	F	1872	r	1905	k	1935	u	1965	k
1842	G	1873	s	1906	l	1936	A	1966	l
1843	H	1874	t	1907	m	1937	B	1967	m
1844	J	1875	u	1908	n	1938	C	1968	n
1845	K	1876	A	1909	o	1939	D	1969	o
1846	L	1877	B	1910	P	1940	E	1970	P
1847	M	1878	C	1911	Q	1941	F	1971	q
1848	N	1879	D	1912	R	1942	G	1972	r
1849	O	1880	E	1913	S	1943	H	1973	s
1850	P	1881	F	1914	t	1944	I	1974	t
1851	Q	1882	G	1915	u	1945	K	1975	A
1852	R	1883	H	1916	a	1946	L	1976	B
1853	S	1884	I	1917	b	1947	M	1977	C
1854	T	1885	K	1918	c	1948	N		
1855	U	1886	L	1919	d	1949	O		
1856	a	1887	M						
		1888	N						
		1889	O						

London hallmarks.

Examples of complete marks (from top to bottom).

Brittania silver made in United Kingdom by Nathaniel Lock and marked in London during the year 1705-1706.

Sterling silver made in United Kingdom by Robert Bowman and marked in Edinburgh during the year 1780-1781.

Sterling silver made in United Kingdom by Robert Duncan and marked in Glasgow (Town mark: tree, bird, bell, fish and ring, city arms) during the year 1819-1820 after plate duty had been paid.

Sterling silver made in United Kingdom by William Dodge and marked in Chester during the year 1864-1865 after plate duty had been paid.

Sterling silver made in United Kingdom by NM and marked in Edinburgh during the year 1935 with the special mark commemorating the silver jubilee of King George V and Queen Mary.

The standard work on the subject is *English Goldsmiths and Their Marks* by Sir Charles J. Jackson. The book contains over thirteen thousand marks.

Hallmarks of other countries, particularly those used by the French authorities, are a complex study and do not necessarily provide an indication of date.

Duty Mark

In 1784 an excise duty on gold and silver ware was introduced. The duty was collected by the assay offices, and as evidence of payment the head of the reigning sovereign was struck as part of the hallmark, two examples of which are shown below. This duty was abolished in 1798 for watch cases but continued until 1890 for general plate before it was completely abolished.

George III

Victoria

To determine the date of hallmarking one must first identify the assay office from the town mark and then refer to the list of letters used by that office until the date letter in question has been found.

STANDARD MARKS - GOLD		
	22 carat Marked in England	1544 — 1843
	22 carat Marked in England	1844 — 1974
	22 carat Marked in Scotland	1844 — 1974
	18 carat Marked in England	1798 — 1974
	18 carat Marked in Scotland	1798 — 1974
	9 carat	1854 — 1974
	12 carat	1854 — 1932 then abolished
	15 carat	1854 — 1932 then abolished)
	14 carat	1932 — 1974

STANDARD MARKS - SILVER	
	Sterling silver Marked in England
	Sterling silver Marked in Scotland
	Brittania silver

APPENDIX 4
Bibliography

Books

G.H. Baillie	Britten's Old Clocks and Watches and Their Makers (Nearly 14,000 names of makers. Well illustrated)	8th ed. 1973	Eyre Methuen in association with E. & F. Spon Ltd. 11 New Fetter Lane London EC4P 4EE
G.H. Baillie	Watchmakers and Clock Makers of the World (35,000 names of mak-ers)	1966	N.A.G. Press Ltd. Northwood House
93-99 GoswellRoad			London, ECIV 7QA
P.M. Chamberlain	It's About Time (The development of escapements. Well illustrated)	1941	R.R. Smith, New York, New York, now, William L. Bauhan, Inc., Old Country Road Dublin, New Hampshire 03444
Cecil Clutton and George Daniels	Watches (577 photographs)	1965	B.T. Batsford Ltd. 4 Fitzhardinge St. Portman Square London, W.1
		1965	Viking Press, Inc. 625 Madison Ave. New York
T.P. Camerer Cuss	The Camerer Cuss Book of Antique Watches (200 photographs)	1976	The Antique Collectors Club Clopton, Woodbridge, Suffolk, England

251

Donald de Carle	Watch and Clock Ency-clopedia (3,000 entries; 1,400 illustrations)	1976	N.A.G. Press Ltd. Northwood House 93-99 Goswell Road London, ECIV 7QA
W.J. Gazeley	Watch and Clock Making and Repairing (Well illustrated repair book)	2nd ed. 1965	Heywood Books 88 Kingsway London, W.C. 2B 6AB
Sir Charles J. Jackson	English Goldsmiths and Their Marks	1964	Dover Publications, Inc., 180 Varick St. New York, New York 10014
			Macmillan & Co. Ltd., Little Essex St., London, W.C.2, England

Journals

American Horologist & Jeweler
    2403 Champa Street
    Denver, Colorado 80205

Antiquarian Horology
    Available to members only. Applications to:
    The Antiquarian Horological Society
    New House
    High Street
    Ticehurst
    Wadhurst
    Sussex TN5 7AL, England

Bulletin of the National Association of Watch and Clock Collectors, Inc.
    Available to members only. Applications to:
    N.A.W.C.C.
    P.O. Box 33
    Columbia, Pennsylvania 17512
    In addition, this author, H.G. Harris, has written three books: Handbook of Watch and Clock Repairs (Revised Edition 1972), Advanced Watch and Clock Repair (1973), and Collecting and Identifying Old Clocks (1977); published by Emerson Books, Inc., Buchanan, New York 10511.

Acknowledgments

The illustrations in this book were made available only by the generous help of others.

I am particularly grateful to Mr. David Evans, a well known horological consultant, for allowing part of his private collection to be photographed and for kindly sparing the time to provide the technical details.

My special thanks go to Mr. Christopher Wood, the notable chronometer specialist, who took the trouble to photograph some of his own instruments and provide their history.

My appreciation for their help is extended to Uto Auktions AG and to Stephen Bogoff for supplying photographs that have appeared in their excellent auction catalogues.

My thanks go also to the London Assay Office for allowing me to reproduce designs of hallmarks published by The Worshipful Company of Goldsmiths.

Finally, I wish to thank Mr. Richard Lonergan for producing the line drawings.

Figs. 11, 28, 29, 30, 44, 45, 46, 47, 48, 49, 50, 51, 52, 53, 54, 55, 56, 66, 70, 71, 72, 73, 74, 76, and 81 by courtesy of Evans & Evans, 41 Broad Street, Alresford, Hampshire SO24 9AS, England.

Figs. 35, 36, 37, 39, 40, 41 and 42 by courtesy of Mr. Christopher Wood, 37 Colinton Road, Edinburgh 10, Scotland.

Figs. 5, 12, 16, 17, 20, 22, 31, 38, 43, 67, 68, 69, 75 and 78 by courtesy of Uto Auktions AG, CH-8027 Zurich, Postfach 568, Laverstrasse 11, Switzerland.

Fig. 8 by courtesy of Bogoff Antique Watch Auction, San Francisco, Ca.

Hallmark designs by courtesy of the Assay Office, Goldsmiths' Hall, Gutter Lane, London EC2V 8AQ.

Color plates I, II, III, IV and V by courtesy of Uto Auktions AG.

INDEX